<u>Disclaimer</u>

Book Title: Guide to Industrial Control Systems (ICS) Security - Supervisory Control and Data Acquisition (SCADA) systems, Distributed Control Systems (DCS), and other control system configurations such as Programmable Logic Controllers (PLC)

Book Author: Keith A. Stouffer; Joseph A. Falco; Karen A. Scarfone

Book Abstract: NIST Special Publication (SP) 800-82, Guide to Industrial Control Systems (ICS) Security, provides guidance on how to secure Industrial Control Systems (ICS), including Supervisory Control and Data Acquisition (SCADA) systems, Distributed Control Systems (DCS), and other control system configurations such as Programmable Logic Controllers (PLC), while addressing their unique performance, reliability, and safety requirements. SP 800-82 provides an overview of ICS and typical system topologies, identifies typical threats and vulnerabilities to these systems, and provides recommended security countermeasures to mitigate the associated risks.

Citation: NIST SP - 800-82

Keyword: Industrial control systems (ICS); IT security; supervisory control and data acquisition (SCADA); distributed control systems (DCS); programmable logic controllers (PLC); FISMA; cyber security

National Institute of
Standards and Technology
U.S. Department of Commerce

Special Publication 800-82

Guide to Industrial Control Systems (ICS) Security

Supervisory Control and Data Acquisition (SCADA) systems, Distributed Control Systems (DCS), and other control system configurations such as Programmable Logic Controllers (PLC)

Recommendations of the National Institute of Standards and Technology

Keith Stouffer
Joe Falco
Karen Scarfone

NIST Special Publication 800-82

Guide to Industrial Control Systems (ICS) Security
Supervisory Control and Data Acquisition (SCADA) systems, Distributed Control Systems (DCS), and other control system configurations such as Programmable Logic Controllers (PLC)

Recommendations of the National Institute of Standards and Technology

C O M P U T E R   S E C U R I T Y

Computer Security Division
Information Technology Laboratory
National Institute of Standards and Technology
Gaithersburg, MD 20899-8930

Intelligent Systems Division
Engineering Laboratory
National Institute of Standards and Technology
Gaithersburg, MD 20899-8930

June 2011

U.S. Department of Commerce

Gary Locke, Secretary

National Institute of Standards and Technology

Patrick Gallagher, Director

Reports on Computer Systems Technology

The Information Technology Laboratory (ITL) at the National Institute of Standards and Technology (NIST) promotes the U.S. economy and public welfare by providing technical leadership for the nation's measurement and standards infrastructure. ITL develops tests, test methods, reference data, proof of concept implementations, and technical analysis to advance the development and productive use of information technology. ITL's responsibilities include the development of technical, physical, administrative, and management standards and guidelines for the cost-effective security and privacy of sensitive unclassified information in Federal computer systems. This Special Publication 800-series reports on ITL's research, guidance, and outreach efforts in computer security and its collaborative activities with industry, government, and academic organizations.

National Institute of Standards and Technology Special Publication 800-82
Natl. Inst. Stand. Technol. Spec. Publ. 800-82, 155 pages (June 2011)

This version superceded by http://dx.doi.org/10.6028/NIST.SP.800-82r1

Acknowledgments

The authors, Keith Stouffer, Joe Falco, and Karen Scarfone of the National Institute of Standards and Technology (NIST), wish to thank their colleagues who reviewed drafts of this document and contributed to its technical content. The authors would particularly like to acknowledge Tim Grance, Ron Ross, Stu Katzke, and Freemon Johnson of NIST for their keen and insightful assistance throughout the development of the document. The authors also gratefully acknowledge and appreciate the many contributions from the public and private sectors whose thoughtful and constructive comments improved the quality and usefulness of this publication. The authors would particularly like to thank the members of ISA99. The authors would also like to thank the UK National Centre for the Protection of National Infrastructure (CPNI)) for allowing portions of the *Good Practice Guide on Firewall Deployment for SCADA and Process Control Network* to be used in this document as well as ISA for allowing portions of the ANSI/ISA99 Standards to be used in this document.

Table of Contents

List of Appendices

List of Figures

List of Tables

Executive Summary

This document provides guidance for establishing secure industrial control systems (ICS). These ICS, which include supervisory control and data acquisition (SCADA) systems, distributed control systems (DCS), and other control system configurations such as skid-mounted Programmable Logic Controllers (PLC) are often found in the industrial control sectors. ICS are typically used in industries such as electric, water and wastewater, oil and natural gas, transportation, chemical, pharmaceutical, pulp and paper, food and beverage, and discrete manufacturing (e.g., automotive, aerospace, and durable goods.) SCADA systems are generally used to control dispersed assets using centralized data acquisition and supervisory control. DCS are generally used to control production systems within a local area such as a factory using supervisory and regulatory control. PLCs are generally used for discrete control for specific applications and generally provide regulatory control. These control systems are vital to the operation of the U.S. critical infrastructures that are often highly interconnected and mutually dependent systems. It is important to note that approximately 90 percent of the nation's critical infrastructures are privately owned and operated. Federal agencies also operate many of the ICS mentioned above; other examples include air traffic control and materials handling (e.g., Postal Service mail handling.) This document provides an overview of these ICS and typical system topologies, identifies typical threats and vulnerabilities to these systems, and provides recommended security countermeasures to mitigate the associated risks.

Initially, ICS had little resemblance to traditional information technology (IT) systems in that ICS were isolated systems running proprietary control protocols using specialized hardware and software. Widely available, low-cost Internet Protocol (IP) devices are now replacing proprietary solutions, which increases the possibility of cyber security vulnerabilities and incidents. As ICS are adopting IT solutions to promote corporate business systems connectivity and remote access capabilities, and are being designed and implemented using industry standard computers, operating systems (OS) and network protocols, they are starting to resemble IT systems. This integration supports new IT capabilities, but it provides significantly less isolation for ICS from the outside world than predecessor systems, creating a greater need to secure these systems. While security solutions have been designed to deal with these security issues in typical IT systems, special precautions must be taken when introducing these same solutions to ICS environments. In some cases, new security solutions are needed that are tailored to the ICS environment.

Although some characteristics are similar, ICS also have characteristics that differ from traditional information processing systems. Many of these differences stem from the fact that logic executing in ICS has a direct affect on the physical world. Some of these characteristics include significant risk to the health and safety of human lives and serious damage to the environment, as well as serious financial issues such as production losses, negative impact to a nation's economy, and compromise of proprietary information. ICS have unique performance and reliability requirements and often use operating systems and applications that may be considered unconventional to typical IT personnel. Furthermore, the goals of safety and efficiency sometimes conflict with security in the design and operation of control systems.

Originally, ICS implementations were susceptible primarily to local threats because many of their components were in physically secured areas and the components were not connected to IT networks or systems. However, the trend toward integrating ICS systems with IT networks provides significantly less isolation for ICS from the outside world than predecessor systems, creating a greater need to secure these systems from remote, external threats. Also, the increasing use of wireless networking places ICS implementations at greater risk from adversaries who are in relatively close physical proximity but do not have direct physical access to the equipment. Threats to control systems can come from numerous sources, including hostile governments, terrorist groups, disgruntled employees, malicious intruders, complexities, accidents, natural disasters as well as malicious or accidental actions by insiders. ICS security objectives typically follow the priority of availability, integrity and confidentiality, in that order.

1

Possible incidents an ICS may face include the following:

Blocked or delayed flow of information through ICS networks, which could disrupt ICS operation

Unauthorized changes to instructions, commands, or alarm thresholds, which could damage, disable, or shut down equipment, create environmental impacts, and/or endanger human life

Inaccurate information sent to system operators, either to disguise unauthorized changes, or to cause the operators to initiate inappropriate actions, which could have various negative effects

ICS software or configuration settings modified, or ICS software infected with malware, which could have various negative effects

Interference with the operation of safety systems, which could endanger human life.

Major security objectives for an ICS implementation should include the following:

Restricting logical access to the ICS network and network activity. This includes using a demilitarized zone (DMZ) network architecture with firewalls to prevent network traffic from passing directly between the corporate and ICS networks, and having separate authentication mechanisms and credentials for users of the corporate and ICS networks. The ICS should also use a network topology that has multiple layers, with the most critical communications occurring in the most secure and reliable layer.

Restricting physical access to the ICS network and devices. Unauthorized physical access to components could cause serious disruption of the ICS's functionality. A combination of physical access controls should be used, such as locks, card readers, and/or guards.

Protecting individual ICS components from exploitation. This includes deploying security patches in as expeditious a manner as possible, after testing them under field conditions; disabling all unused ports and services; restricting ICS user privileges to only those that are required for each person's role; tracking and monitoring audit trails; and using security controls such as antivirus software and file integrity checking software where technically feasible to prevent, deter, detect, and mitigate malware.

Maintaining functionality during adverse conditions. This involves designing the ICS so that each critical component has a redundant counterpart. Additionally, if a component fails, it should fail in a manner that does not generate unnecessary traffic on the ICS or other networks, or does not cause another problem elsewhere, such as a cascading event.

Restoring system after an incident. Incidents are inevitable and an incident response plan is essential. A major characteristic of a good security program is how quickly a system can be recovered after an incident has occurred.

To properly address security in an ICS, it is essential for a cross-functional cyber security team to share their varied domain knowledge and experience to evaluate and mitigate risk to the ICS. The cyber security team should consist of a member of the organization's IT staff, control engineer, control system operator, network and system security expert, a member of the management staff, and a member of the physical security department at a minimum. For continuity and completeness, the cyber security team should consult with the control system vendor and/or system integrator as well. The cyber security team should report directly to site management (e.g., facility superintendent) or the company's CIO/CSO, who in turn, accepts complete responsibility and accountability for the cyber security of the ICS. An effective cyber security program for an ICS should apply a strategy known as "defense-in-depth", layering security mechanisms such that the impact of a failure in any one mechanism is minimized.

In a typical ICS this means a defense-in-depth strategy that includes:

Developing security policies, procedures, training and educational material that apply specifically to the ICS.

Considering ICS security policies and procedures based on the Homeland Security Advisory System Threat Level, deploying increasingly heightened security postures as the Threat Level increases.

Addressing security throughout the lifecycle of the ICS from architecture design to procurement to installation to maintenance to decommissioning.

Implementing a network topology for the ICS that has multiple layers, with the most critical communications occurring in the most secure and reliable layer.

Providing logical separation between the corporate and ICS networks (e.g., stateful inspection firewall(s) between the networks).

Employing a DMZ network architecture (i.e., prevent direct traffic between the corporate and ICS networks).

Ensuring that critical components are redundant and are on redundant networks.

Designing critical systems for graceful degradation (fault tolerant) to prevent catastrophic cascading events.

Disabling unused ports and services on ICS devices after testing to assure this will not impact ICS operation.

Restricting physical access to the ICS network and devices.

Restricting ICS user privileges to only those that are required to perform each person's job (i.e., establishing role-based access control and configuring each role based on the principle of least privilege).

Considering the use of separate authentication mechanisms and credentials for users of the ICS network and the corporate network (i.e., ICS network accounts do not use corporate network user accounts).

Using modern technology, such as smart cards for Personal Identity Verification (PIV).

Implementing security controls such as intrusion detection software, antivirus software and file integrity checking software, where technically feasible, to prevent, deter, detect, and mitigate the introduction, exposure, and propagation of malicious software to, within, and from the ICS.

Applying security techniques such as encryption and/or cryptographic hashes to ICS data storage and communications where determined appropriate.

Expeditiously deploying security patches after testing all patches under field conditions on a test system if possible, before installation on the ICS.

Tracking and monitoring audit trails on critical areas of the ICS.

NIST has created the Industrial Control System Security project[1] in cooperation with the public and private sector ICS community to develop specific guidance on the application of the security controls in NIST SP 800-53, *Recommended Security Controls for Federal Information Systems and Organizations* to ICS.

While most controls in Appendix F of NIST SP 800-53 are applicable to ICS as written, several controls did require ICS-specific interpretation and/or augmentation by adding one or more of the following to the control:

> ~~ICS Supplemental Guidance~~ provides organizations with additional information on the application of the security controls and control enhancements in Appendix F of NIST SP 800-53 to ICS and the environments in which these specialized systems operate. The Supplemental Guidance also provides information as to why a particular security control or control enhancement may not be applicable in some ICS environments and may be a candidate for tailoring (i.e., the application of scoping guidance and/or compensating controls). ICS Supplemental Guidance does not replace the original Supplemental Guidance in Appendix F of NIST SP 800-53.
>
> ~~ICS Enhancements~~ (one or more) that provide enhancement augmentations to the original control that may be required for some ICS
>
> ~~ICS Enhancement Supplemental Guidance~~ that provides guidance on how the control enhancement applies, or does not apply, in ICS environments.

This ICS-specific guidance is included in NIST SP 800-53, Revision 3, Appendix I: Industrial Control Systems – Security Controls, Enhancements, and Supplemental Guidance. Section 6 of this document also provides initial guidance on how 800-53 security controls apply to ICS. Initial recommendations and guidance, if available, are provided in an outlined box for each section. NIST is planning a December 2011 update to NIST SP 800-53 (NIST SP 800-53, Revision 4), including an update of current security controls, control enhancements, supplemental guidance, as well as tailoring and supplementation guidance, in the area of industrial control systems.

Additionally, Appendix C of this document provides an overview of the many activities currently ongoing among Federal organizations, standards organizations, industry groups, and automation system vendors to make available recommended practices in the area of ICS security.

> The most successful method for securing an ICS is to gather industry recommended practices and engage in a proactive, collaborative effort between management, the controls engineer and operator, the IT organization, and a trusted automation advisor. This team should draw upon the wealth of information available from ongoing federal government, industry groups, vendor and standards organizational activities listed in Appendix C.

---

[1] The Industrial Control System Security Project Web site is located at: ~~http://csrc.nist.gov/groups/SMA/fismalics/~~

1. Introduction

1.1 Authority

The National Institute of Standards and Technology (NIST) developed this document in furtherance of its statutory responsibilities under the Federal Information Security Management Act (FISMA) of 2002, Public Law 107-347 and Homeland Security Presidential Directive 7 (HSPD-7) of 2003.

NIST is responsible for developing standards and guidelines, including minimum requirements, for providing adequate information security for all agency operations and assets, but such standards and guidelines shall not apply to national security systems. This guideline is consistent with the requirements of the Office of Management and Budget (OMB) Circular A-130, Section 8b(3), "Securing Agency Information Systems," as analyzed in A-130, Appendix IV: Analysis of Key Sections. Supplemental information is provided in A-130, Appendix III.

This guideline has been prepared for use by Federal agencies. It may be used by nongovernmental organizations on a voluntary basis and is not subject to copyright, though attribution is desired.

Nothing in this document should be taken to contradict standards and guidelines made mandatory and binding on Federal agencies by the Secretary of Commerce under statutory authority, nor should these guidelines be interpreted as altering or superseding the existing authorities of the Secretary of Commerce, Director of the OMB, or any other Federal official.

1.2 Purpose and Scope

The purpose of this document is to provide guidance for securing industrial control systems (ICS), including supervisory control and data acquisition (SCADA) systems, distributed control systems (DCS), and other systems performing control functions. The document provides an overview of ICS and typical system topologies, identifies typical threats and vulnerabilities to these systems, and provides recommended security countermeasures to mitigate the associated risks. Because there are many different types of ICS with varying levels of potential risk and impact, the document provides a list of many different methods and techniques for securing ICS. The document should not be used purely as a checklist to secure a specific system. Readers are encouraged to perform a risk-based assessment on their systems and to tailor the recommended guidelines and solutions to meet their specific security, business and operational requirements.

The scope of this document includes ICS that are typically used in the electric, water and wastewater, oil and natural gas, chemical, pharmaceutical, pulp and paper, food and beverage, and discrete manufacturing (automotive, aerospace, and durable goods) industries.

1.3 Audience

This document covers details specific to ICS. The document is technical in nature; however, it provides the necessary background to understand the topics that are discussed.

The intended audience is varied and includes the following:

Control engineers, integrators, and architects who design or implement secure ICS

System administrators, engineers, and other information technology (IT) professionals who administer, patch, or secure ICS

Security consultants who perform security assessments and penetration testing of ICS

Managers who are responsible for ICS

Senior management who are trying to understand implications and consequences as they justify and apply an ICS cyber security program to help mitigate impacts to business functionality

Researchers and analysts who are trying to understand the unique security needs of ICS

Vendors that are developing products that will be deployed as part of an ICS

Readers of this document are assumed to be familiar with general computer security concepts, communication protocols such as those used in networking and with using Web-based methods for retrieving information.

1.4 Document Structure

The remainder of this guide is divided into the following major sections:

Section 2 provides an overview of SCADA and other ICS as well as their importance as a rationale for the need for security.

Section 3 provides a discussion of differences between ICS and IT systems, as well as threats, vulnerabilities and incidents.

Section 4 provides an overview of the development and deployment of an ICS security program to mitigate the risk of the vulnerabilities identified in Section 3.

Section 5 provides recommendations for integrating security into network architectures typically found in ICS, with an emphasis on network segregation practices.

Section 6 provides a summary of the management, operational, and technical controls identified in NIST Special Publication 800-53, *Recommended Security Controls for Federal Information Systems and Organizations*, and provides initial guidance on how these security controls apply to ICS.

The guide also contains several appendices with supporting material, as follows:

Appendix A provides a list of acronyms and abbreviations used in this document.

Appendix B provides a glossary of terms used in this document.

Appendix C provides a list and short description of some of the current activities in ICS security.

Appendix D provides a list of some emerging security capabilities being developed for ICS.

Appendix E provides an overview of the FISMA implementation project and supporting documents, and the relevancy of FISMA to ICS.

Appendix F provides a list of references used in the development of this document.

2. Overview of Industrial Control Systems

Industrial control system (ICS) is a general term that encompasses several types of control systems, including supervisory control and data acquisition (SCADA) systems, distributed control systems (DCS), and other control system configurations such as skid-mounted Programmable Logic Controllers (PLC) often found in the industrial sectors and critical infrastructures. ICS are typically used in industries such as electrical, water and wastewater, oil and natural gas, chemical, transportation, pharmaceutical, pulp and paper, food and beverage, and discrete manufacturing (e.g., automotive, aerospace, and durable goods.) These control systems are critical to the operation of the U.S. critical infrastructures that are often highly interconnected and mutually dependent systems. It is important to note that approximately 90 percent of the nation's critical infrastructures are privately owned and operated. Federal agencies also operate many of the industrial processes mentioned above; other examples include air traffic control and materials handling (e.g., Postal Service mail handling.) This section provides an overview of SCADA, DCS, and PLC systems, including typical architectures and components. Several diagrams are presented to depict the network connections and components typically found on each system to facilitate the understanding of these systems. Keep in mind that actual implementations of ICS may be hybrids that blur the line between DCS and SCADA systems by incorporating attributes of both. Please note that the diagrams in this section do not represent a secure ICS. Architecture security and security controls are discussed in Section 5 and Section 6 of this document respectively.

2.1 Overview of SCADA, DCS, and PLCs

SCADA systems are highly distributed systems used to control geographically dispersed assets, often scattered over thousands of square kilometers, where centralized data acquisition and control are critical to system operation. They are used in distribution systems such as water distribution and wastewater collection systems, oil and natural gas pipelines, electrical power grids, and railway transportation systems. A SCADA control center performs centralized monitoring and control for field sites over long-distance communications networks, including monitoring alarms and processing status data. Based on information received from remote stations, automated or operator-driven supervisory commands can be pushed to remote station control devices, which are often referred to as field devices. Field devices control local operations such as opening and closing valves and breakers, collecting data from sensor systems, and monitoring the local environment for alarm conditions.

DCS are used to control industrial processes such as electric power generation, oil refineries, water and wastewater treatment, and chemical, food, and automotive production. DCS are integrated as a control architecture containing a supervisory level of control overseeing multiple, integrated sub-systems that are responsible for controlling the details of a localized process. Product and process control are usually achieved by deploying feed back or feed forward control loops whereby key product and/or process conditions are automatically maintained around a desired set point. To accomplish the desired product and/or process tolerance around a specified set point, specific PLCs are employed in the field and proportional, integral, and/or derivative settings on the PLC are tuned to provide the desired tolerance as well as the rate of self-correction during process upsets. DCS are used extensively in process-based industries.

PLCs are computer-based solid-state devices that control industrial equipment and processes. While PLCs are control system components used throughout SCADA and DCS systems, they are often the primary components in smaller control system configurations used to provide operational control of discrete processes such as automobile assembly lines and power plant soot blower controls. PLCs are used extensively in almost all industrial processes.

The process-based manufacturing industries typically utilize two main processes [1]:

Continuous Manufacturing Processes. These processes run continuously, often with transitions to make different grades of a product. Typical continuous manufacturing processes include fuel or steam flow in a power plant, petroleum in a refinery, and distillation in a chemical plant.

Batch Manufacturing Processes. These processes have distinct processing steps, conducted on a quantity of material. There is a distinct start and end step to a batch process with the possibility of brief steady state operations during intermediate steps. Typical batch manufacturing processes include food manufacturing.

The discrete-based manufacturing industries typically conduct a series of steps on a single device to create the end product. Electronic and mechanical parts assembly and parts machining are typical examples of this type of industry.

Both process-based and discrete-based industries utilize the same types of control systems, sensors, and networks. Some facilities are a hybrid of discrete and process-based manufacturing.

While control systems used in distribution and manufacturing industries are very similar in operation, they are different in some aspects. One of the primary differences is that DCS or PLC-controlled sub-systems are usually located within a more confined factory or plant-centric area, when compared to geographically dispersed SCADA field sites. DCS and PLC communications are usually performed using local area network (LAN) technologies that are typically more reliable and high speed compared to the long-distance communication systems used by SCADA systems. In fact, SCADA systems are specifically designed to handle long-distance communication challenges such as delays and data loss posed by the various communication media used. DCS and PLC systems usually employ greater degrees of closed loop control than SCADA systems because the control of industrial processes is typically more complicated than the supervisory control of distribution processes. These differences can be considered subtle for the scope of this document, which focuses on the integration of IT security into these systems. Throughout the remainder of this document, SCADA systems, DCS and PLC systems will be referred to as ICS unless a specific reference is made to one (e.g., field device used in a SCADA system).

2.2 ICS Operation

The basic operation of an ICS is shown in Figure 2-1 [2]. Key components include the following:

Control Loop. A control loop consists of sensors for measurement, controller hardware such as PLCs, actuators such as control valves, breakers, switches and motors, and the communication of variables. Controlled variables are transmitted to the controller from the sensors. The controller interprets the signals and generates corresponding manipulated variables, based on set points, which it transmits to the actuators. Process changes from disturbances result in new sensor signals, identifying the state of the process, to again be transmitted to the controller.

Human-Machine Interface (HMI). Operators and engineers use HMIs to monitor and configure set points, control algorithms, and adjust and establish parameters in the controller. The HMI also displays process status information and historical information.

Remote Diagnostics and Maintenance Utilities. Diagnostics and maintenance utilities are used to prevent, identify and recover from abnormal operation or failures.

A typical ICS contains a proliferation of control loops, HMIs, and remote diagnostics and maintenance tools built using an array of network protocols on layered network architectures. Sometimes these control loops are nested and/or cascading –whereby the set point for one loop is based on the process variable determined by another loop. Supervisory-level loops and lower-level loops operate continuously over the duration of a process with cycle times ranging on the order of milliseconds to minutes.

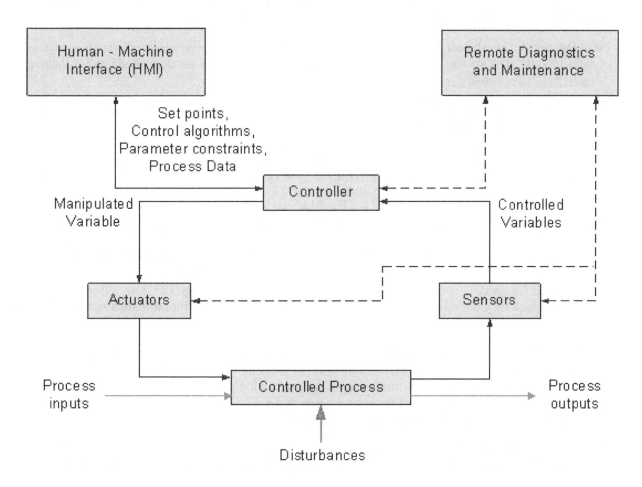

Figure 2-1. ICS Operation

2.3 Key ICS Components

To support subsequent discussions, this section defines key ICS components that are used in control and networking. Some of these components can be described generically for use in SCADA systems, DCS and PLCs, while others are unique to one. The Glossary of Terms in Appendix B contains a more detailed listing of control and networking components. Additionally, Figure 2-5 and Figure 2-6 in Section 2.4 show SCADA implementation examples, Figure 2-7 in Section 2.5 shows a DCS implementation example and Figure 2-8 in Section 2.6 shows a PLC system implementation example that incorporates these components.

2.3.1 Control Components

The following is a list of the major control components of an ICS:

Control Server. The control server hosts the DCS or PLC supervisory control software that communicates with lower-level control devices. The control server accesses subordinate control modules over an ICS network.

SCADA Server or Master Terminal Unit (MTU). The SCADA Server is the device that acts as the master in a SCADA system. Remote terminal units and PLC devices (as described below) located at remote field sites usually act as slaves.

Remote Terminal Unit (RTU). The RTU, also called a remote telemetry unit, is a special purpose data acquisition and control unit designed to support SCADA remote stations. RTUs are field devices often equipped with wireless radio interfaces to support remote situations where wire-based communications are unavailable. Sometimes PLCs are implemented as field devices to serve as RTUs; in this case, the PLC is often referred to as an RTU.

Programmable Logic Controller (PLC). The PLC is a small industrial computer originally designed to perform the logic functions executed by electrical hardware (relays, switches, and mechanical timer/counters). PLCs have evolved into controllers with the capability of controlling complex processes, and they are used substantially in SCADA systems and DCS. Other controllers used at the field level are process controllers and RTUs; they provide the same control as PLCs but are designed for specific control applications. In SCADA environments, PLCs are often used as field devices because they are more economical, versatile, flexible, and configurable than special-purpose RTUs.

Intelligent Electronic Devices (IED). An IED is a "smart" sensor/actuator containing the intelligence required to acquire data, communicate to other devices, and perform local processing and control. An IED could combine an analog input sensor, analog output, low-level control capabilities, a communication system, and program memory in one device. The use of IEDs in SCADA and DCS systems allows for automatic control at the local level.

Human-Machine Interface (HMI). The HMI is software and hardware that allows human operators to monitor the state of a process under control, modify control settings to change the control objective, and manually override automatic control operations in the event of an emergency. The HMI also allows a control engineer or operator to configure set points or control algorithms and parameters in the controller. The HMI also displays process status information, historical information, reports, and other information to operators, administrators, managers, business partners, and other authorized users. The location, platform, and interface may vary a great deal. For example, an HMI could be a dedicated platform in the control center, a laptop on a wireless LAN, or a browser on any system connected to the Internet.

Data Historian. The data historian is a centralized database for logging all process information within an ICS. Information stored in this database can be accessed to support various analyses, from statistical process control to enterprise level planning.

Input/Output (IO) Server. The IO server is a control component responsible for collecting, buffering and providing access to process information from control sub-components such as PLCs, RTUs and IEDs. An IO server can reside on the control server or on a separate computer platform. IO servers are also used for interfacing third-party control components, such as an HMI and a control server.

2.3.2 Network Components

There are different network characteristics for each layer within a control system hierarchy. Network topologies across different ICS implementations vary with modern systems using Internet-based IT and enterprise integration strategies. Control networks have merged with corporate networks to allow control engineers to monitor and control systems from outside of the control system network. The connection may also allow enterprise-level decision-makers to obtain access to process data. The following is a list of the major components of an ICS network, regardless of the network topologies in use:

Fieldbus Network. The fieldbus network links sensors and other devices to a PLC or other controller. Use of fieldbus technologies eliminates the need for point-to-point wiring between the controller and each device. The devices communicate with the fieldbus controller using a variety of protocols. The messages sent between the sensors and the controller uniquely identify each of the sensors.

Control Network. The control network connects the supervisory control level to lower-level control modules.

Communications Routers. A router is a communications device that transfers messages between two networks. Common uses for routers include connecting a LAN to a WAN, and connecting MTUs and RTUs to a long-distance network medium for SCADA communication.

Firewall. A firewall protects devices on a network by monitoring and controlling communication packets using predefined filtering policies. Firewalls are also useful in managing ICS network segregation strategies.

Modems. A modem is a device used to convert between serial digital data and a signal suitable for transmission over a telephone line to allow devices to communicate. Modems are often used in SCADA systems to enable long-distance serial communications between MTUs and remote field devices. They are also used in SCADA systems, DCS and PLCs for gaining remote access for operational and maintenance functions such as entering commands or modifying parameters, and diagnostic purposes.

Remote Access Points. Remote access points are distinct devices, areas and locations of a control network for remotely configuring control systems and accessing process data. Examples include using a personal digital assistant (PDA) to access data over a LAN through a wireless access point, and using a laptop and modem connection to remotely access an ICS system.

2.4   SCADA Systems

SCADA systems are used to control dispersed assets where centralized data acquisition is as important as control [3] [4]. These systems are used in distribution systems such as water distribution and wastewater collection systems, oil and natural gas pipelines, electrical utility transmission and distribution systems, and rail and other public transportation systems. SCADA systems integrate data acquisition systems with data transmission systems and HMI software to provide a centralized monitoring and control system for numerous process inputs and outputs. SCADA systems are designed to collect field information, transfer it to a central computer facility, and display the information to the operator graphically or textually, thereby allowing the operator to monitor or control an entire system from a central location in real time. Based on the sophistication and setup of the individual system, control of any individual system, operation, or task can be automatic, or it can be performed by operator commands.

SCADA systems consist of both hardware and software. Typical hardware includes an MTU placed at a control center, communications equipment (e.g., radio, telephone line, cable, or satellite), and one or more geographically distributed field sites consisting of either an RTU or a PLC, which controls actuators and/or monitors sensors. The MTU stores and processes the information from RTU inputs and outputs, while the RTU or PLC controls the local process. The communications hardware allows the transfer of information and data back and forth between the MTU and the RTUs or PLCs. The software is programmed to tell the system what and when to monitor, what parameter ranges are acceptable, and what response to initiate when parameters change outside acceptable values. An IED, such as a protective relay, may communicate directly to the SCADA Server, or a local RTU may poll the IEDs to collect the data and pass it to the SCADA Server. IEDs provide a direct interface to control and monitor equipment and sensors. IEDs may be directly polled and controlled by the SCADA Server and in most cases have local programming that allows for the IED to act without direct instructions from the SCADA control center. SCADA systems are usually designed to be fault-tolerant systems with significant redundancy built into the system architecture.

Figure 2-2 shows the components and general configuration of a SCADA system. The control center houses a SCADA Server (MTU) and the communications routers. Other control center components include the HMI, engineering workstations, and the data historian, which are all connected by a LAN. The control center collects and logs information gathered by the field sites, displays information to the HMI, and may generate actions based upon detected events. The control center is also responsible for centralized alarming, trend analyses, and reporting. The field site performs local control of actuators and monitors sensors. Field sites are often equipped with a remote access capability to allow field operators to perform remote diagnostics and repairs usually over a separate dial up modem or WAN connection. Standard and proprietary communication protocols running over serial communications are used to transport information between the control center and field sites using telemetry techniques such as telephone line, cable, fiber, and radio frequency such as broadcast, microwave and satellite.

MTU-RTU communication architectures vary among implementations. The various architectures used, including point-to-point, series, series-star, and multi-drop [5], are shown in Figure 2-3. Point-to-point is functionally the simplest type; however, it is expensive because of the individual channels needed for each connection. In a series configuration, the number of channels used is reduced; however, channel sharing has an impact on the efficiency and complexity of SCADA operations. Similarly, the series-star and multi-drop configurations' use of one channel per device results in decreased efficiency and increased system complexity.

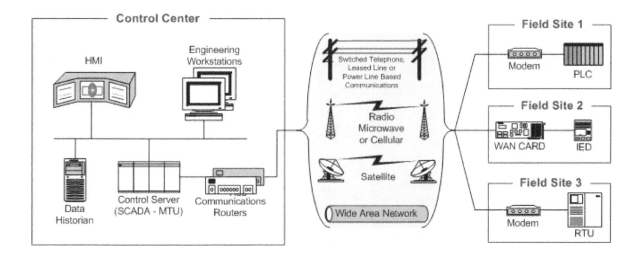

Figure 2-2. SCADA System General Layout

The four basic architectures shown in Figure 2-3 can be further augmented using dedicated communication devices to manage communication exchange as well as message switching and buffering. Large SCADA systems, containing hundreds of RTUs, often employ sub-MTUs to alleviate the burden on the primary MTU. This type of topology is shown in Figure 2-4.

Figure 2-5 shows an example of a SCADA system implementation. This particular SCADA system consists of a primary control center and three field sites. A second backup control center provides redundancy in the event of a primary control center malfunction. Point-to-point connections are used for all control center to field site communications, with two connections using radio telemetry. The third field site is local to the control center and uses the wide area network (WAN) for communications. A regional control center resides above the primary control center for a higher level of supervisory control. The corporate network has access to all control centers through the WAN, and field sites can be accessed remotely for troubleshooting and maintenance operations. The primary control center polls field devices for data at defined intervals (e.g., 5 seconds, 60 seconds) and can send new set points to a field device as required. In addition to polling and issuing high-level commands, the SCADA server also watches for priority interrupts coming from field site alarm systems.

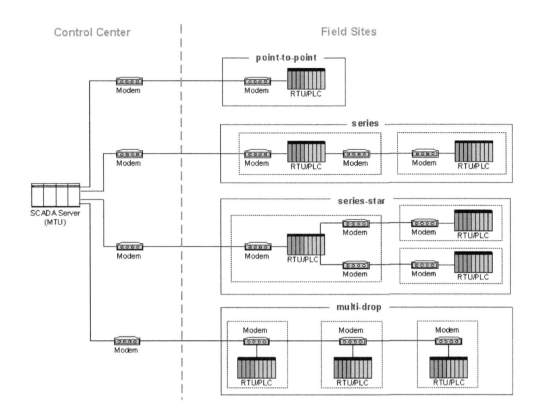

Figure 2-3. Basic SCADA Communication Topologies

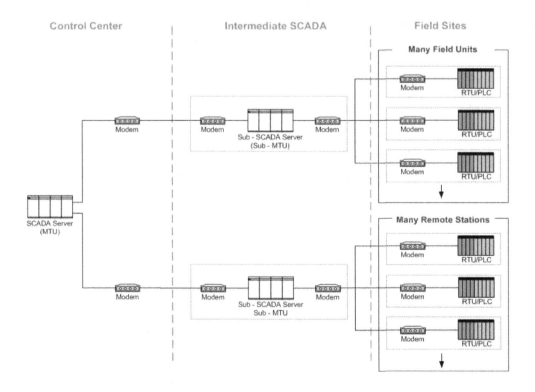

Figure 2-4. Large SCADA Communication Topology

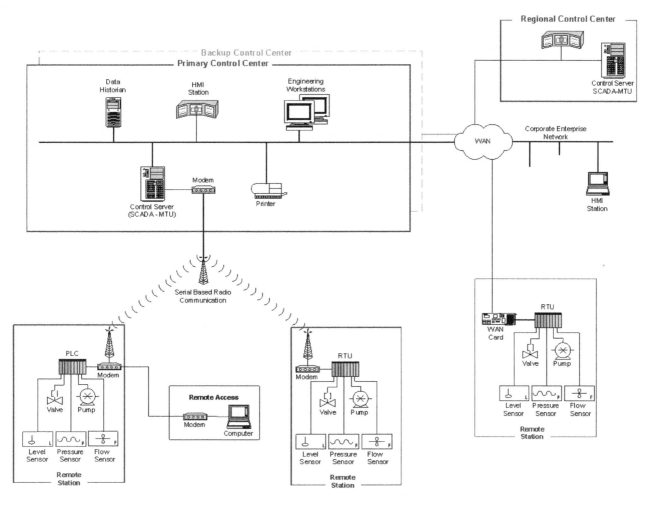

Figure 2-5. SCADA System Implementation Example (Distribution Monitoring and Control)

Figure 2-6 shows an example implementation for rail monitoring and control. This example includes a rail control center that houses the SCADA system and three sections of a rail system. The SCADA system polls the rail sections for information such as the status of the trains, signal systems, traction electrification systems, and ticket vending machines. This information is also fed to operator consoles at the HMI station within the rail control center. The SCADA system also monitors operator inputs at the rail control center and disperses high-level operator commands to the rail section components. In addition, the SCADA system monitors conditions at the individual rail sections and issues commands based on these conditions (e.g., shut down a train to prevent it from entering an area that has been determined to be flooded or occupied by another train based on condition monitoring).

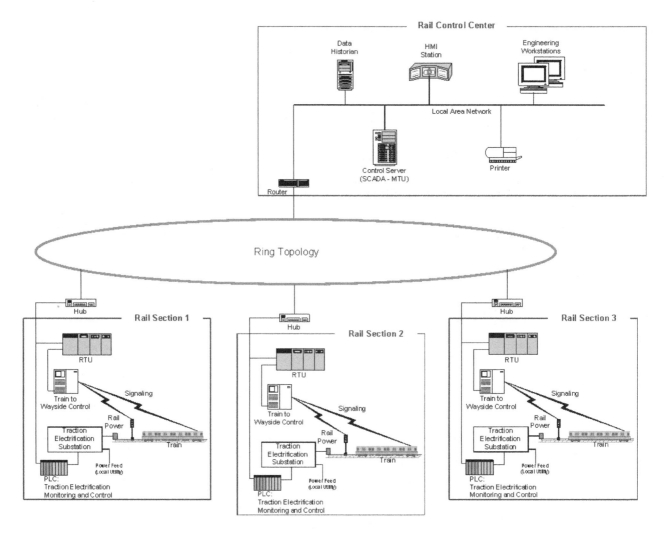

Figure 2-6. SCADA System Implementation Example (Rail Monitoring and Control)

2.5   Distributed Control Systems

DCS are used to control production systems within the same geographic location for industries such as oil refineries, water and wastewater treatment, electric power generation plants, chemical manufacturing plants, and pharmaceutical processing facilities. These systems are usually process control or discrete part control systems. A DCS uses a centralized supervisory control loop to mediate a group of localized controllers that share the overall tasks of carrying out an entire production process [6]. By modularizing the production system, a DCS reduces the impact of a single fault on the overall system. In many modern systems, the DCS is interfaced with the corporate network to give business operations a view of production.

An example implementation showing the components and general configuration of a DCS is depicted in Figure 2-7. This DCS encompasses an entire facility from the bottom-level production processes up to the corporate or enterprise layer. In this example, a supervisory controller (control server) communicates to its subordinates via a control network. The supervisor sends set points to and requests data from the distributed field controllers. The distributed controllers control their process actuators based on control server commands and sensor feedback from process sensors.

Figure 2-7 gives examples of low-level controllers found on a DCS system. The field control devices shown include a PLC, a process controller, a single loop controller, and a machine controller. The single loop controller interfaces sensors and actuators using point-to-point wiring, while the other three field devices incorporate fieldbus networks to interface with process sensors and actuators. Fieldbus networks eliminate the need for point-to-point wiring between a controller and individual field sensors and actuators. Additionally, a fieldbus allows greater functionality beyond control, including field device diagnostics, and can accomplish control algorithms within the fieldbus, thereby avoiding signal routing back to the PLC for every control operation. Standard industrial communication protocols designed by industry groups such as Modbus and Fieldbus [7] are often used on control networks and fieldbus networks.

In addition to the supervisory-level and field-level control loops, intermediate levels of control may also exist. For example, in the case of a DCS controlling a discrete part manufacturing facility, there could be an intermediate level supervisor for each cell within the plant. This supervisor would encompass a manufacturing cell containing a machine controller that processes a part and a robot controller that handles raw stock and final products. There could be several of these cells that manage field-level controllers under the main DCS supervisory control loop.

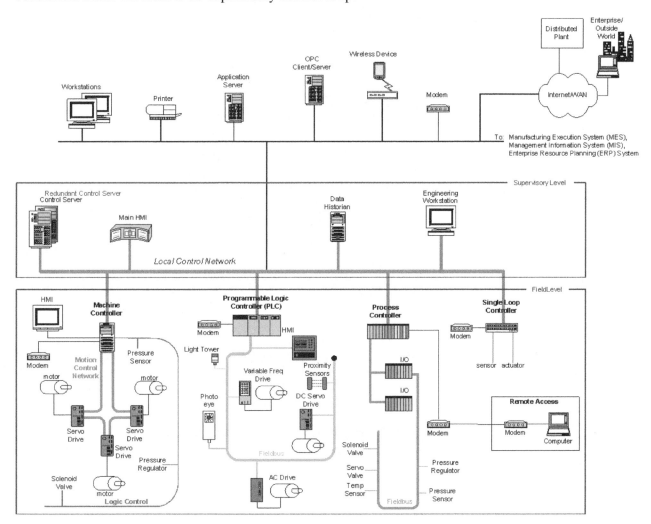

Figure 2-7. DCS Implementation Example

2.6   Programmable Logic Controllers

PLCs are used in both SCADA and DCS systems as the control components of an overall hierarchical system to provide local management of processes through feedback control as described in the sections above. In the case of SCADA systems, they provide the same functionality of RTUs. When used in DCS, PLCs are implemented as local controllers within a supervisory control scheme. PLCs are also implemented as the primary components in smaller control system configurations. PLCs have a user-programmable memory for storing instructions for the purpose of implementing specific functions such as I/O control, logic, timing, counting, three mode proportional-integral-derivative (PID) control, communication, arithmetic, and data and file processing. Figure 2-8 shows control of a manufacturing process being performed by a PLC over a fieldbus network. The PLC is accessible via a programming interface located on an engineering workstation, and data is stored in a data historian, all connected on a LAN.

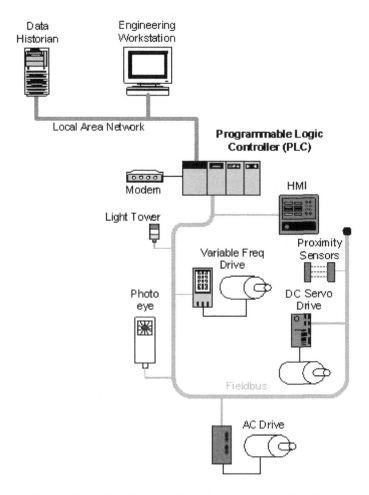

Figure 2-8. PLC Control System Implementation Example

2.7   Industrial Sectors and Their Interdependencies

Both the electrical power transmission and distribution grid industries use geographically distributed SCADA control technology to operate highly interconnected and dynamic systems consisting of thousands of public and private utilities and rural cooperatives for supplying electricity to end users. SCADA systems monitor and control electricity distribution by collecting data from and issuing commands to geographically remote field control stations from a centralized location. SCADA systems are also used to monitor and control water, oil and natural gas distribution, including pipelines, ships, trucks, and rail systems, as well as wastewater collection systems.

SCADA systems and DCS are often networked together. This is the case for electric power control centers and electric power generation facilities. Although the electric power generation facility operation is controlled by a DCS, the DCS must communicate with the SCADA system to coordinate production output with transmission and distribution demands.

The U.S. critical infrastructure is often referred to as a "system of systems" because of the interdependencies that exist between its various industrial sectors as well as interconnections between business partners [8] [9]. Critical infrastructures are highly interconnected and mutually dependent in complex ways, both physically and through a host of information and communications technologies. An incident in one infrastructure can directly and indirectly affect other infrastructures through cascading and escalating failures.

Electric power is often thought to be one of the most prevalent sources of disruptions of interdependent critical infrastructures. As an example, a cascading failure can be initiated by a disruption of the microwave communications network used for an electric power transmission SCADA system. The lack of monitoring and control capabilities could cause a large generating unit to be taken offline, an event that would lead to loss of power at a transmission substation. This loss could cause a major imbalance, triggering a cascading failure across the power grid. This could result in large area blackouts that could potentially affect oil and natural gas production, refinery operations, water treatment systems, wastewater collection systems, and pipeline transport systems that rely on the grid for electric power.

3. ICS Characteristics, Threats and Vulnerabilities

Most ICS in use today were developed years ago, long before public and private networks, desktop computing, or the Internet were a common part of business operations. These systems were designed to meet performance, reliability, safety, and flexibility requirements. In most cases they were physically isolated from outside networks and based on proprietary hardware, software, and communication protocols that included basic error detection and correction capabilities, but lacked the secure communication capabilities required in today's interconnected systems. While there was concern for Reliability, Maintainability, and Availability (RMA) when addressing statistical performance and failure, the need for cyber security measures within these systems was not anticipated. At the time, security for ICS meant physically securing access to the network and the consoles that controlled the systems.

ICS development paralleled the evolution of microprocessor, personal computer, and networking technologies during the 1980's and 1990's, and Internet-based technologies started making their way into ICS designs in the late 1990's. These changes to ICS exposed them to new types of threats and significantly increased the likelihood that ICS could be compromised. This section describes the unique security characteristics of ICS, the vulnerabilities in ICS implementations, and the threats and incidents that ICS may face. Section 3.7 presents several examples of actual ICS cyber security incidents.

3.1 Comparing ICS and IT Systems

Initially, ICS had little resemblance to IT systems in that ICS were isolated systems running proprietary control protocols using specialized hardware and software. Widely available, low-cost Internet Protocol (IP) devices are now replacing proprietary solutions, which increases the possibility of cyber security vulnerabilities and incidents. As ICS are adopting IT solutions to promote corporate connectivity and remote access capabilities, and are being designed and implemented using industry standard computers, operating systems (OS) and network protocols, they are starting to resemble IT systems. This integration supports new IT capabilities, but it provides significantly less isolation for ICS from the outside world than predecessor systems, creating a greater need to secure these systems. While security solutions have been designed to deal with these security issues in typical IT systems, special precautions must be taken when introducing these same solutions to ICS environments. In some cases, new security solutions are needed that are tailored to the ICS environment.

ICS have many characteristics that differ from traditional IT systems, including different risks and priorities. Some of these include significant risk to the health and safety of human lives, serious damage to the environment, and financial issues such as production losses, and negative impact to a nation's economy. ICS have different performance and reliability requirements and use operating systems and applications that may be considered unconventional to typical IT support personnel. Furthermore, the goals of safety and efficiency can sometimes conflict with security in the design and operation of control systems (e.g., requiring password authentication and authorization should not hamper or interfere with emergency actions for ICS.) The following lists some special considerations when considering security for ICS:

> **Performance Requirements.** ICS are generally time-critical, with the criterion for acceptable levels of delay and jitter dictated by the individual installation. Some systems require deterministic responses. High throughput is typically not essential to ICS. In contrast, IT systems typically require high throughput, and they can typically withstand some level of delay and jitter
>
> **Availability Requirements.** Many ICS processes are continuous in nature. Unexpected outages of systems that control industrial processes are not acceptable. Outages often must be planned and scheduled days/weeks in advance. Exhaustive pre-deployment testing is essential to ensure high

availability for the ICS. In addition to unexpected outages, many control systems cannot be easily stopped and started without affecting production. In some cases, the products being produced or equipment being used is more important than the information being relayed. Therefore, the use of typical IT strategies such as rebooting a component, are usually not acceptable solutions due to the adverse impact on the requirements for high availability, reliability and maintainability of the ICS. Some ICS employ redundant components, often running in parallel, to provide continuity when primary components are unavailable.

Risk Management Requirements. In a typical IT system, data confidentiality and integrity are typically the primary concerns. For an ICS, human safety and fault tolerance to prevent loss of life or endangerment of public health or confidence, regulatory compliance, loss of equipment, loss of intellectual property, or lost or damaged products are the primary concerns. The personnel responsible for operating, securing, and maintaining ICS must understand the important link between safety and security.

Architecture Security Focus. In a typical IT system, the primary focus of security is protecting the operation of IT assets, whether centralized or distributed, and the information stored on or transmitted among these assets. In some architectures, information stored and processed centrally is more critical and is afforded more protection. For ICS, edge clients (e.g., PLC, operator station, DCS controller) need to be carefully protected because they are directly responsible for controlling the end processes. The protection of the central server is still very important in an ICS, because the central server could possibly adversely impact every edge device.

Physical Interaction. In a typical IT system, there is not physical interaction with the environment. ICS can have very complex interactions with physical processes and consequences in the ICS domain that can manifest in physical events. All security functions integrated into the ICS must be tested (e.g., off-line on a comparable ICS) to prove that they do not compromise normal ICS functionality.

Time-Critical Responses. In a typical IT system, access control can be implemented without significant regard for data flow. For some ICS, automated response time or system response to human interaction is very critical. For example, requiring password authentication and authorization on an HMI must not hamper or interfere with emergency actions for ICS. Information flow must not be interrupted or compromised. Access to these systems should be restricted by rigorous physical security controls.

System Operation. ICS operating systems (OS) and applications may not tolerate typical IT security practices. Legacy systems are especially vulnerable to resource unavailability and timing disruptions. Control networks are often more complex and require a different level of expertise (e.g., control networks are typically managed by control engineers, not IT personnel). Software and hardware are more difficult to upgrade in an operational control system network. Many systems may not have desired features including encryption capabilities, error logging, and password protection.

Resource Constraints. ICS and their real time OSs are often resource-constrained systems that usually do not include typical IT security capabilities. There may not be computing resources available on ICS components to retrofit these systems with current security capabilities. Additionally, in some instances, third-party security solutions are not allowed due to ICS vendor license and service agreements, and loss of service support can occur if third party applications are installed without vendor acknowledgement or approval.

Communications. Communication protocols and media used by ICS environments for field device control and intra-processor communication are typically different from the generic IT environment, and may be proprietary.

Change Management. Change management is paramount to maintaining the integrity of both IT and control systems. Unpatched software represents one of the greatest vulnerabilities to a system. Software updates on IT systems, including security patches, are typically applied in a timely fashion based on appropriate security policy and procedures. In addition, these procedures are often automated using server-based tools. Software updates on ICS cannot always be implemented on a timely basis because these updates need to be thoroughly tested by the vendor of the industrial control application and the end user of the application before being implemented and ICS outages often must be planned and scheduled days/weeks in advance. The ICS may also require revalidation as part of the update process. Another issue is that many ICS utilize older versions of operating systems that are no longer supported by the vendor. Consequently, available patches may not be applicable. Change management is also applicable to hardware and firmware. The change management process, when applied to ICS, requires careful assessment by ICS experts (e.g., control engineers) working in conjunction with security and IT personnel.

Managed Support. Typical IT systems allow for diversified support styles, perhaps supporting disparate but interconnected technology architectures. For ICS, service support is usually via a single vendor, which may not have a diversified and interoperable support solution from another vendor.

Component Lifetime. Typical IT components have a lifetime on the order of 3 to 5 years, with brevity due to the quick evolution of technology. For ICS where technology has been developed in many cases for very specific use and implementation, the lifetime of the deployed technology is often in the order of 15 to 20 years and sometimes longer.

Access to Components. Typical IT components are usually local and easy to access, while ICS components can be isolated, remote, and require extensive physical effort to gain access to them.

Table 3-1 summarizes some of the typical differences between IT systems and ICS.

Table 3-1. Summary of IT System and ICS Differences

Category	Information Technology System	Industrial Control System
Performance Requirements	Non-real-time	Real-time
	Response must be consistent	Response is time-critical
	High throughput is demanded	Modest throughput is acceptable
	High delay and jitter may be acceptable	High delay and/or jitter is not acceptable
Availability Requirements	Responses such as rebooting are acceptable	Responses such as rebooting may not be acceptable because of process availability requirements
	Availability deficiencies can often be tolerated, depending on the system's operational requirements	Availability requirements may necessitate redundant systems
		Outages must be planned and scheduled days/weeks in advance
		High availability requires exhaustive pre-deployment testing

Category	Information Technology System	Industrial Control System
Risk Management Requirements	Data confidentiality and integrity is paramount Fault tolerance is less important – momentary downtime is not a major risk Major risk impact is delay of business operations	Human safety is paramount, followed by protection of the process Fault tolerance is essential, even momentary downtime may not be acceptable Major risk impacts are regulatory non-compliance, environmental impacts, loss of life, equipment, or production
Architecture Security Focus	Primary focus is protecting the IT assets, and the information stored on or transmitted among these assets. Central server may require more protection	Primary goal is to protect edge clients (e.g., field devices such as process controllers) Protection of central server is also important
Unintended Consequences	Security solutions are designed around typical IT systems	Security tools must be tested (e.g., off-line on a comparable ICS) to ensure that they do not compromise normal ICS operation
Time-Critical Interaction	Less critical emergency interaction Tightly restricted access control can be implemented to the degree necessary for security	Response to human and other emergency interaction is critical Access to ICS should be strictly controlled, but should not hamper or interfere with human-machine interaction
System Operation	Systems are designed for use with typical operating systems Upgrades are straightforward with the availability of automated deployment tools	Differing and possibly proprietary operating systems, often without security capabilities built in Software changes must be carefully made, usually by software vendors, because of the specialized control algorithms and perhaps modified hardware and software involved
Resource Constraints	Systems are specified with enough resources to support the addition of third-party applications such as security solutions	Systems are designed to support the intended industrial process and may not have enough memory and computing resources to support the addition of security capabilities
Communications	Standard communications protocols Primarily wired networks with some localized wireless capabilities Typical IT networking practices	Many proprietary and standard communication protocols Several types of communications media used including dedicated wire and wireless (radio and satellite) Networks are complex and sometimes require the expertise of control engineers
Change Management	Software changes are applied in a timely fashion in the presence of good security policy and procedures. The procedures are often automated.	Software changes must be thoroughly tested and deployed incrementally throughout a system to ensure that the integrity of the control system is maintained. ICS outages often must be planned and scheduled days/weeks in advance. ICS may use OSs that are no longer supported
Managed Support	Allow for diversified support styles	Service support is usually via a single vendor
Component Lifetime	Lifetime on the order of 3-5 years	Lifetime on the order of 15-20 years
Access to Components	Components are usually local and easy to access	Components can be isolated, remote, and require extensive physical effort to gain access to them

Available computing resources for ICS (including central processing unit [CPU] time and memory) tend to be very limited because these systems were designed to maximize control system resources, with little to no extra capacity for third-party cyber security solutions. Additionally, in some instances, third-party security solutions are not allowed due to vendor license and service agreements, and loss of service support can occur if third party applications are installed. Another important consideration is that IT cyber security and control systems expertise is typically not found within the same group of personnel.

In summary, the operational and risk differences between ICS and IT systems create the need for increased sophistication in applying cyber security and operational strategies. A cross-functional team of control engineers, control system operators and IT security professionals needs to work closely to understand the possible implications of the installation, operation, and maintenance of security solutions in conjunction with control system operation. IT professionals working with ICS need to understand the reliability impacts of information security technologies before deployment. Some of the OSs and applications running on ICS may not operate correctly with commercial-off-the-shelf (COTS) IT cyber security solutions because of specialized ICS environment architectures.

3.2 Threats

Threats to control systems can come from numerous sources, including adversarial sources such as hostile governments, terrorist groups, industrial spies, disgruntled employees, malicious intruders, and natural sources such as from system complexities, human errors and accidents, equipment failures and natural disasters. To protect against adversarial threats (as well as known natural threats), it is necessary to create a defense-in-depth strategy for the ICS. Table 3-2 lists possible threats to ICS. Please note this list is in alphabetical order and not by greatest threat.

Table 3-2. Adversarial Threats to ICS

Threat Agent	Description
Attackers	Attackers break into networks for the thrill of the challenge or for bragging rights in the attacker community. While remote cracking once required a fair amount of skill or computer knowledge, attackers can now download attack scripts and protocols from the Internet and launch them against victim sites. Thus, while attack tools have become more sophisticated, they have also become easier to use. Many attackers do not have the requisite expertise to threaten difficult targets such as critical U.S. networks. Nevertheless, the worldwide population of attackers poses a relatively high threat of an isolated or brief disruption causing serious damage.
Bot-network operators	Bot-network operators are attackers; however, instead of breaking into systems for the challenge or bragging rights, they take over multiple systems to coordinate attacks and to distribute phishing schemes, spam, and malware attacks. The services of compromised systems and networks are sometimes made available on underground markets (e.g., purchasing a denial of service attack or the use of servers to relay spam or phishing attacks).
Criminal groups	Criminal groups seek to attack systems for monetary gain. Specifically, organized crime groups are using spam, phishing, and spyware/malware to commit identity theft and online fraud. International corporate spies and organized crime organizations also pose a threat to the U.S. through their ability to conduct industrial espionage and large-scale monetary theft and to hire or develop attacker talent. Some criminal groups may try to extort money from an organization by threatening a cyber attack.

Threat Agent	Description
Foreign intelligence services	Foreign intelligence services use cyber tools as part of their information gathering and espionage activities. In addition, several nations are aggressively working to develop information warfare doctrines, programs, and capabilities. Such capabilities enable a single entity to have a significant and serious impact by disrupting the supply, communications, and economic infrastructures that support military power – impacts that could affect the daily lives of U.S. citizens.
Insiders	The disgruntled insider is a principal source of computer crime. Insiders may not need a great deal of knowledge about computer intrusions because their knowledge of a target system often allows them to gain unrestricted access to cause damage to the system or to steal system data. The insider threat also includes outsourcing vendors as well as employees who accidentally introduce malware into systems. Insiders may be employees, contractors, or business partners. Inadequate policies, procedures, and testing can, and have led to ICS impacts. Impacts have ranged from trivial to significant damage to the ICS and field devices. Unintentional impacts from insiders are some of the highest probability occurrences.
Phishers	Phishers are individuals or small groups that execute phishing schemes in an attempt to steal identities or information for monetary gain. Phishers may also use spam and spyware/malware to accomplish their objectives.
Spammers	Spammers are individuals or organizations that distribute unsolicited e-mail with hidden or false information to sell products, conduct phishing schemes, distribute spyware/malware, or attack organizations (e.g., DoS).
Spyware/malware authors	Individuals or organizations with malicious intent carry out attacks against users by producing and distributing spyware and malware. Several destructive computer viruses and worms have harmed files and hard drives, including the Melissa Macro Virus, the Explore.Zip worm, the CIH (Chernobyl) Virus, Nimda, Code Red, Slammer, and Blaster.
Terrorists	Terrorists seek to destroy, incapacitate, or exploit critical infrastructures to threaten national security, cause mass casualties, weaken the U.S. economy, and damage public morale and confidence. Terrorists may use phishing schemes or spyware/malware to generate funds or gather sensitive information. Terrorists may attack one target to divert attention or resources from other targets.
Industrial spies	Industrial espionage seeks to acquire intellectual property and know-how by clandestine methods

Source: Government Accountability Office (GAO), Department of Homeland Security's (DHS's) Role in Critical Infrastructure Protection (CIP) Cybersecurity, GAO-05-434 (Washington, D.C.: May, 2005).

3.3 Potential ICS Vulnerabilities

This section lists vulnerabilities that may be found in typical ICS. The order of these vulnerabilities does not necessarily reflect any priority in terms of likelihood of occurrence or severity of impact. The vulnerabilities are grouped into Policy and Procedure, Platform, and Network categories to assist in determining optimal mitigation strategies. Any given ICS will usually exhibit a subset of these vulnerabilities, but may also contain additional vulnerabilities unique to the particular ICS implementation that do not appear in this listing. Specific information on ICS vulnerabilities can be researched at the United States Computer Emergency Readiness Team (US-CERT) Control Systems Web site.[2]

When studying possible security vulnerabilities, it is easy to become preoccupied with trying to address issues that are technically interesting, but are ultimately of low impact. As addressed in Appendix E,

---

[2] The US-CERT Control Systems Web site is located at http://www.us-cert.gov/control_systems/

FIPS 199 establishes security categories for both information and information systems based on the potential impact on an organization should certain events occur which jeopardize the information and information systems needed by the organization to accomplish its assigned mission, protect its assets, fulfill its legal responsibilities, maintain its day-to-day functions, and protect individuals.

A method for assessing and rating the risk of a possible vulnerability at a specific facility is needed. The risk is a function of the likelihood (probability) that a defined threat agent (adversary) can exploit a specific vulnerability and create an impact (consequence). The risk induced by any given vulnerability is influenced by a number of related indicators, including:

Network and computer architecture and conditions

Installed countermeasures

Technical difficulty of the attack

Probability of detection (e.g., amount of time the adversary can remain in contact with the target system/network without detection)

Consequences of the incident

Cost of the incident.

This assessment of risk is addressed in further detail in Sections 4 through 6.

3.3.1 Policy and Procedure Vulnerabilities

Vulnerabilities are often introduced into ICS because of incomplete, inappropriate, or nonexistent security documentation, including policy and implementation guides (procedures). Security documentation, along with management support, is the cornerstone of any security program. Corporate security policy can reduce vulnerabilities by mandating conduct such as password usage and maintenance or requirements for connecting modems to ICS. Table 3-3 describes potential policy and procedure vulnerabilities for ICS.

Table 3-3. Policy and Procedure Vulnerabilities

Vulnerability	Description
Inadequate security policy for the ICS	Vulnerabilities are often introduced into ICS due to inadequate policies or the lack of policies specifically for control system security.
No formal ICS security training and awareness program	A documented formal security training and awareness program is designed to keep staff up to date on organizational security policies and procedures as well as industry cyber security standards and recommended practices. Without training on specific ICS policies and procedures, staff cannot be expected to maintain a secure ICS environment.
Inadequate security architecture and design	Control engineers have historically had minimal training in security and until relatively recently vendors have not included security features in their products
No specific or documented security procedures were developed from the security policy for the ICS	Specific security procedures should be developed and employees trained for the ICS. They are the roots of a sound security program.
Absent or deficient ICS equipment implementation guidelines	Equipment implementation guidelines should be kept up to date and readily available. These guidelines are an integral part of security procedures in the event of an ICS malfunction.
Lack of administrative mechanisms for security enforcement	Staff responsible for enforcing security should be held accountable for administering documented security policies and procedures.

Vulnerability	Description
Few or no security audits on the ICS	Independent security audits should review and examine a system's records and activities to determine the adequacy of system controls and ensure compliance with established ICS security policy and procedures. Audits should also be used to detect breaches in ICS security services and recommend changes, which may include making existing security controls more robust and/or adding new security controls.
No ICS specific continuity of operations or disaster recovery plan (DRP)	A DRP should be prepared, tested and available in the event of a major hardware or software failure or destruction of facilities. Lack of a specific DRP for the ICS could lead to extended downtimes and production loss.
Lack of ICS specific configuration change management	A process for controlling modifications to hardware, firmware, software, and documentation should be implemented to ensure an ICS is protected against inadequate or improper modifications before, during, and after system implementation. A lack of configuration change management procedures can lead to security oversights, exposures, and risks.

3.3.2 Platform Vulnerabilities

Vulnerabilities in ICS can occur due to flaws, misconfigurations, or poor maintenance of their platforms, including hardware, operating systems, and ICS applications. These vulnerabilities can be mitigated through various security controls, such as OS and application patching, physical access control, and security software (e.g., antivirus software). The tables in this section describe potential platform vulnerabilities:

Table 3-4. Platform Configuration Vulnerabilities

Table 3-5. Platform Hardware Vulnerabilities

Table 3-6. Platform Software Vulnerabilities

Table 3-7. Platform Malware Protection Vulnerabilities

Table 3-4. Platform Configuration Vulnerabilities

Vulnerability	Description
OS and vendor software patches may not be developed until significantly after security vulnerabilities are found	Because of the complexity of ICS software and possible modifications to the underlying OS, changes must undergo comprehensive regression testing. The elapsed time for such testing and subsequent distribution of updated software provides a long window of vulnerability
OS and application security patches are not maintained	Out-of-date OSs and applications may contain newly discovered vulnerabilities that could be exploited. Documented procedures should be developed for how security patches will be maintained. Security patch support may not even be available for ICS that use outdated OSs.
OS and application security patches are implemented without exhaustive testing	OS and application security patches deployed without testing could compromise normal operation of the ICS. Documented procedures should be developed for testing new security patches.
Default configurations are used	Using default configurations often leads to insecure and unnecessary open ports and exploitable services and applications running on hosts.
Critical configurations are not stored or backed up	Procedures should be available for restoring ICS configuration settings in the event of accidental or adversary-initiated configuration changes to maintain system availability and prevent loss of data. Documented procedures should be developed for maintaining ICS configuration settings.

Vulnerability	Description
Data unprotected on portable device	If sensitive data (e.g., passwords, dial-up numbers) is stored in the clear on portable devices such as laptops and PDAs and these devices are lost or stolen, system security could be compromised. Policy, procedures, and mechanisms are required for protection.
Lack of adequate password policy	Password policies are needed to define when passwords must be used, how strong they must be, and how they must be maintained. Without a password policy, systems might not have appropriate password controls, making unauthorized access to systems more likely. Password policies should be developed as part of an overall ICS security program taking into account the capabilities of the ICS and its personnel to handle more complex passwords.
No password used	Passwords should be implemented on ICS components to prevent unauthorized access. Password-related vulnerabilities include having no password for: • System login (if the system has user accounts) • System power-on (if the system has no user accounts) • System screen saver (if an ICS component is unattended over time) Password authentication should not hamper or interfere with emergency actions for ICS.
Password disclosure	Passwords should be kept confidential to prevent unauthorized access. Examples of password disclosures include: • Posting passwords in plain sight, local to a system • Sharing passwords to individual user accounts with associates • Communicating passwords to adversaries through social engineering • Sending passwords that are not encrypted through unprotected communications
Password guessing	Poorly chosen passwords can easily be guessed by humans or computer algorithms to gain unauthorized access. Examples include: • Passwords that are short, simple (e.g., all lower-case letters), or otherwise do not meet typical strength requirements. Password strength also depends on the specific ICS capability to handle more stringent passwords • Passwords that are left as the default vendor supplied value • Passwords that are not changed on a specified interval
Inadequate access controls applied	Poorly specified access controls can result in giving an ICS user too many or too few privileges. The following exemplify each case: • System configured with default access control settings gives an operator administrative privileges • System improperly configured results in an operator being unable to take corrective actions in an emergency situation Access control policies should be developed as part of an ICS security program.

Table 3-5. Platform Hardware Vulnerabilities

Vulnerability	Description
Inadequate testing of security changes	Many ICS facilities, especially smaller facilities, have no test facilities, so security changes must be implemented using the live operational systems
Inadequate physical protection for critical systems	Access to the control center, field devices, portable devices, media, and other ICS components needs to be controlled. Many remote sites are often not staffed and it may not be feasible to physically monitor them.
Unauthorized personnel have physical access to equipment	Physical access to ICS equipment should be restricted to only the necessary personnel, taking into account safety requirements, such as emergency shutdown or restarts. Improper access to ICS equipment can lead to any of the following: • Physical theft of data and hardware • Physical damage or destruction of data and hardware • Unauthorized changes to the functional environment (e.g., data connections, unauthorized use of removable media, adding/removing resources) • Disconnection of physical data links • Undetectable interception of data (keystroke and other input logging)
Insecure remote access on ICS components	Modems and other remote access capabilities that enable control engineers and vendors to gain remote access to systems should be deployed with security controls to prevent unauthorized individuals from gaining access to the ICS.
Dual network interface cards (NIC) to connect networks	Machines with dual NICs connected to different networks could allow unauthorized access and passing of data from one network to another.
Undocumented assets	To properly secure an ICS, there should be an accurate listing of the assets in the system. An inaccurate representation of the control system and its components could leave an unauthorized access point or backdoor into the ICS.
Radio frequency and electro-magnetic pulse (EMP)	The hardware used for control systems is vulnerable to radio frequency and electro-magnetic pulses (EMP). The impact can range from temporary disruption of command and control to permanent damage to circuit boards.
Lack of backup power	Without backup power to critical assets, a general loss of power will shut down the ICS and could create an unsafe situation. Loss of power could also lead to insecure default settings.
Loss of environmental control	Loss of environmental control could lead to processors overheating. Some processors will shut down to protect themselves; some may continue to operate but in a minimal capacity, producing intermittent errors; and some just melt if they overheat.
Lack of redundancy for critical components	Lack of redundancy in critical components could provide single point of failure possibilities

Table 3-6. Platform Software Vulnerabilities

Vulnerability	Description
Buffer overflow	Software used to implement an ICS could be vulnerable to buffer overflows; adversaries could exploit these to perform various attacks.
Installed security capabilities not enabled by default	Security capabilities that were installed with the product are useless if they are not enabled or at least identified as being disabled.
Denial of service (DoS)	ICS software could be vulnerable to DoS attacks, resulting in the prevention of authorized access to a system resource or delaying system operations and functions.

Vulnerability	Description
Mishandling of undefined, poorly defined, or "illegal" conditions	Some ICS implementations are vulnerable to packets that are malformed or contain illegal or otherwise unexpected field values.
OLE for Process Control (OPC) relies on Remote Procedure Call (RPC) and Distributed Component Object Model (DCOM)	Without updated patches, OPC is vulnerable to the known RPC/DCOM vulnerabilities.
Use of insecure industry-wide ICS protocols	Distributed Network Protocol (DNP) 3.0, Modbus, Profibus, and other protocols are common across several industries and protocol information is freely available. These protocols often have few or no security capabilities built in.
Use of clear text	Many ICS protocols transmit messages in clear text across the transmission media, making them susceptible to eavesdropping by adversaries.
Unneeded services running	Many platforms have a wide variety of processor and network services defined to operate as a default. Unneeded services are seldom disabled and could be exploited.
Use of proprietary software that has been discussed at conferences and in periodicals	Proprietary software issues are discussed at international IT, ICS and "Black Hat" conferences and available through technical papers, periodicals and listservers. Also, ICS maintenance manuals are available from the vendors. This information can help adversaries create successful attacks against ICS.
Inadequate authentication and access control for configuration and programming software	Unauthorized access to configuration and programming software could provide the ability to corrupt a device.
Intrusion detection/prevention software not installed	Incidents can result in loss of system availability; the capture, modification, and deletion of data; and incorrect execution of control commands. IDS/IPS software may stop or prevent various types of attacks, including DoS attacks, and also identify attacked internal hosts, such as those infected with worms. IDS/IPS software must be tested prior to deployment to determine that it does not compromise normal operation of the ICS.
Logs not maintained	Without proper and accurate logs, it might be impossible to determine what caused a security event to occur.
Incidents are not detected	Where logs and other security sensors are installed, they may not be monitored on a real-time basis and therefore security incidents may not be rapidly detected and countered.

Table 3-7. Platform Malware Protection Vulnerabilities

Vulnerability	Description
Malware protection software not installed	Malicious software can result in performance degradation, loss of system availability, and the capture, modification, or deletion of data. Malware protection software, such as antivirus software, is needed to prevent systems from being infected by malicious software.
Malware protection software or definitions not current	Outdated malware protection software and definitions leave the system open to new malware threats.
Malware protection software implemented without exhaustive testing	Malware protection software deployed without testing could impact normal operation of the ICS.

3.3.3 Network Vulnerabilities

Vulnerabilities in ICS may occur from flaws, misconfigurations, or poor administration of ICS networks and their connections with other networks. These vulnerabilities can be eliminated or mitigated through various security controls, such as defense-in-depth network design, encrypting network communications, restricting network traffic flows, and providing physical access control for network components.

The tables in this section describe potential platform vulnerabilities:

Table 3-8. Network Configuration Vulnerabilities

Table 3-9. Network Hardware Vulnerabilities

Table 3-10. Network Perimeter Vulnerabilities

Table 3-11. Network Monitoring and Logging Vulnerabilities

Table 3-12. Communication Vulnerabilities

Table 3-13. Wireless Connection Vulnerabilities

Table 3-8. Network Configuration Vulnerabilities

Vulnerability	Description
Weak network security architecture	The network infrastructure environment within the ICS has often been developed and modified based on business and operational requirements, with little consideration for the potential security impacts of the changes. Over time, security gaps may have been inadvertently introduced within particular portions of the infrastructure. Without remediation, these gaps may represent backdoors into the ICS.
Data flow controls not employed	Data flow controls, such as access control lists (ACL), are needed to restrict which systems can directly access network devices. Generally, only designated network administrators should be able to access such devices directly. Data flow controls should ensure that other systems cannot directly access the devices.
Poorly configured security equipment	Using default configurations often leads to insecure and unnecessary open ports and exploitable network services running on hosts. Improperly configured firewall rules and router ACLs can allow unnecessary traffic.
Network device configurations not stored or backed up	Procedures should be available for restoring network device configuration settings in the event of accidental or adversary-initiated configuration changes to maintain system availability and prevent loss of data. Documented procedures should be developed for maintaining network device configuration settings.
Passwords are not encrypted in transit	Passwords transmitted in clear text across transmission media are susceptible to eavesdropping by adversaries, who could reuse them to gain unauthorized access to a network device. Such access could allow an adversary to disrupt ICS operations or to monitor ICS network activity.
Passwords exist indefinitely on network devices	Passwords should be changed regularly so that if one becomes known by an unauthorized party, the party has unauthorized access to the network device only for a short time. Such access could allow an adversary to disrupt ICS operations or monitor ICS network activity.
Inadequate access controls applied	Unauthorized access to network devices and administrative functions could allow a user to disrupt ICS operations or monitor ICS network activity.

Table 3-9. Network Hardware Vulnerabilities

Vulnerability	Description
Inadequate physical protection of network equipment	Access to network equipment should be controlled to prevent damage or destruction.
Unsecured physical ports	Unsecured universal serial bus (USB) and PS/2 ports could allow unauthorized connection of thumb drives, keystroke loggers, etc.
Loss of environmental control	Loss of environmental control could lead to processors overheating. Some processors will shut down to protect themselves, and some just melt if they overheat.
Non-critical personnel have access to equipment and network connections	Physical access to network equipment should be restricted to only the necessary personnel. Improper access to network equipment can lead to any of the following: • Physical theft of data and hardware • Physical damage or destruction of data and hardware • Unauthorized changes to the security environment (e.g., altering ACLs to permit attacks to enter a network) • Unauthorized interception and manipulation of network activity • Disconnection of physical data links or connection of unauthorized data links
Lack of redundancy for critical networks	Lack of redundancy in critical networks could provide single point of failure possibilities

Table 3-10. Network Perimeter Vulnerabilities

Vulnerability	Description
No security perimeter defined	If the control network does not have a security perimeter clearly defined, then it is not possible to ensure that the necessary security controls are deployed and configured properly. This can lead to unauthorized access to systems and data, as well as other problems.
Firewalls nonexistent or improperly configured	A lack of properly configured firewalls could permit unnecessary data to pass between networks, such as control and corporate networks. This could cause several problems, including allowing attacks and malware to spread between networks, making sensitive data susceptible to monitoring/eavesdropping on the other network, and providing individuals with unauthorized access to systems.
Control networks used for non-control traffic	Control and non-control traffic have different requirements, such as determinism and reliability, so having both types of traffic on a single network makes it more difficult to configure the network so that it meets the requirements of the control traffic. For example, non-control traffic could inadvertently consume resources that control traffic needs, causing disruptions in ICS functions.
Control network services not within the control network	Where IT services such as Domain Name System (DNS),and/or Dynamic Host Configuration Protocol (DHCP) are used by control networks, they are often implemented in the IT network, causing the ICS network to become dependent on the IT network that may not have the reliability and availability requirements needed by the ICS.

Table 3-11. Network Monitoring and Logging Vulnerabilities

Vulnerability	Description
Inadequate firewall and router logs	Without proper and accurate logs, it might be impossible to determine what caused a security incident to occur.
No security monitoring on the ICS network	Without regular security monitoring, incidents might go unnoticed, leading to additional damage and/or disruption. Regular security monitoring is also needed to identify problems with security controls, such as misconfigurations and failures.

Table 3-12. Communication Vulnerabilities

Vulnerability	Description
Critical monitoring and control paths are not identified	Rogue and/or unknown connections into the ICS can leave a backdoor for attacks.
Standard, well-documented communication protocols are used in plain text	Adversaries that can monitor the ICS network activity can use a protocol analyzer or other utilities to decode the data transferred by protocols such as telnet, File Transfer Protocol (FTP), and Network File System (NFS). The use of such protocols also makes it easier for adversaries to perform attacks against the ICS and manipulate ICS network activity.
Authentication of users, data or devices is substandard or nonexistent	Many ICS protocols have no authentication at any level. Without authentication, there is the potential to replay, modify, or spoof data or to spoof devices such as sensors and user identities.
Lack of integrity checking for communications	There are no integrity checks built into most industrial control protocols; adversaries could manipulate communications undetected. To ensure integrity, the ICS can use lower-layer protocols (e.g., IPsec) that offer data integrity protection.

Table 3-13. Wireless Connection Vulnerabilities

Vulnerability	Description
Inadequate authentication between clients and access points	Strong mutual authentication between wireless clients and access points is needed to ensure that clients do not connect to a rogue access point deployed by an adversary, and also to ensure that adversaries do not connect to any of the ICS's wireless networks.
Inadequate data protection between clients and access points	Sensitive data between wireless clients and access points should be protected using strong encryption to ensure that adversaries cannot gain unauthorized access to the unencrypted data.

3.4 Risk Factors

Several factors currently contribute to the increasing risk to control systems, which are discussed in greater detail in Sections 3.4.1 through 3.4.4:

Adoption of standardized protocols and technologies with known vulnerabilities

Connectivity of the control systems to other networks

Insecure and rogue connections

Widespread availability of technical information about control systems.

3.4.1   Standardized Protocols and Technologies

ICS vendors have begun to open up their proprietary protocols and publish their protocol specifications to enable third-party manufacturers to build compatible accessories. Organizations are also transitioning from proprietary systems to less expensive, standardized technologies such as Microsoft Windows and Unix-like operating systems as well as common networking protocols such as TCP/IP to reduce costs and improve performance. Another standard contributing to this evolution of open systems is OPC, a protocol that enables interaction between control systems and PC-based application programs. The transition to using these open protocol standards provides economic and technical benefits, but also increases the susceptibility of ICS to cyber incidents. These standardized protocols and technologies have commonly known vulnerabilities, which are susceptible to sophisticated and effective exploitation tools that are widely available and relatively easy to use.

3.4.2   Increased Connectivity

ICS and corporate IT systems are often interconnected as a result of several changes in information management practices, operational, and business needs. The demand for remote access has encouraged many organizations to establish connections to the ICS that enable ICS engineers and support personnel to monitor and control the system from points outside the control network. Many organizations have also added connections between corporate networks and ICS networks to allow the organization's decision makers to obtain access to critical data about the status of their operational systems and to send instructions for the manufacture or distribution of product. In early implementations this might have been done with custom applications software or via an OPC server/gateway; however, in the past ten years this has been accomplished with Transmission Control Protocol/Internet Protocol (TCP/IP) networking and standardized IP applications like File Transfer Protocol (FTP) or Extensible Markup Language (XML) data exchanges. Often, these connections were implemented without a full understanding of the corresponding security risks. In addition, corporate networks are often connected to strategic partner networks and to the Internet. Control systems also make more use of WANs and the Internet to transmit data to their remote or local stations and individual devices. This integration of control system networks with public and corporate networks increases the accessibility of control system vulnerabilities. Unless appropriate security controls are deployed, these vulnerabilities can expose all levels of the ICS network architecture to complexity-induced error, adversaries and a variety of cyber threats, including worms and other malware. As an example of the change in threats to control systems, an internal survey of an unnamed energy organization showed the following:

The majority of the business units' management believed their control systems were not connected to the corporate network.

An audit showed the majority of the control systems were connected in some way to the corporate network.

The corporate network was only secured to support general business processes and not safety-critical systems.

Adding to the complexity of the situation, the goals of IT departments can be fundamentally different from those of process control departments. The IT world typically sees performance, confidentiality, and data integrity as paramount, while the ICS world sees human and plant safety as its primary responsibility, and thus system availability and data integrity are core priorities. Other distinctions, as discussed in Section 3.1, include differences in reliability requirements, incident impacts, performance expectations, operating systems, communications protocols, and system architectures. This can mean significant differences in implementation of security practices.

3.4.3 Insecure and Rogue Connections

Many ICS vendors have delivered systems with dial-up modems that provide remote access to ease the burdens of maintenance for the technical field support personnel. Remote access sometimes provides support staff with administrative-level access to a system, such as using a telephone number, and sometimes an access control credential (e.g., valid ID, and/or a password). Adversaries with *war dialers*—simple personal computer programs that dial consecutive phone numbers looking for modems— and password cracking software could gain access to systems through these remote access capabilities. Passwords used for remote access are often common to all implementations of a particular vendor's systems and may have not been changed by the end user. These types of connections can leave a system highly vulnerable because people entering systems through vendor-installed modems are often granted high levels of system access.

Organizations often inadvertently leave access links such as dial-up modems open for remote diagnostics, maintenance, and monitoring. Also, control systems increasingly utilize wireless communications systems, which can be vulnerable. Access links not protected with authentication and/or encryption have the increased risk of adversaries using these unsecured connections to access remotely controlled systems. This could lead to an adversary compromising the integrity of the data in transit as well as the availability of the system, both of which can result in an impact to public and plant safety. Before deploying encryption, first determine if encryption is an appropriate solution for the specific ICS application. Section 6.3.4.1 provides additional information on the use of encryption in the ICS environment.

Many of the interconnections between corporate networks and ICS require the integration of systems with different communications standards. The result is often an infrastructure that is engineered to move data successfully between two unique systems. Because of the complexity of integrating disparate systems, control engineers often fail to address the added burden of accounting for security risks. Many control engineers have little if any training in security and often IT security personnel are not involved in ICS security design. As a result, access controls designed to protect control systems from unauthorized access through corporate networks are usually minimal. Moreover, the behavior of the underlying protocols may not be well understood, and thus vulnerabilities can exist that can defeat even advanced security countermeasures. Protocols, such as TCP/IP and others have characteristics that often go unchecked, and this may counter any security that can be done at the network or the application levels.

3.4.4 Public Information

Public information regarding ICS design, maintenance, interconnection, and communication is readily available over the Internet to support competition in product choices as well as to enable the use of open standards. ICS vendors also sell toolkits to help develop software that implements the various standards used in ICS environments. There are also many former employees, vendors, contractors, and other end users of the same ICS equipment worldwide who have inside knowledge about the operation of control systems and processes. For example, one person used his inside knowledge of a system to cause one of the most cited ICS cyber security incidents, the Maroochy Shire sewage spill. Additional information on the Maroochy Shire sewage spill incident is available in Section 3.7.

Information and resources are available to potential adversaries and intruders of all calibers around the world. With the available information, it is quite possible for an individual with very little knowledge of control systems to gain unauthorized access to a control system with the use of automated attack and data mining tools and a factory-set default password. Many times, these default passwords are never changed.

3.5   Possible Incident Scenarios

There are many possible incident scenarios for an ICS including [10]:

Control systems operation disrupted by delaying or blocking the flow of information through corporate or control networks, thereby denying availability of the networks to control system operators or causing information transfer bottlenecks or denial of service by IT-resident services (such as DNS)

Unauthorized changes made to programmed instructions in PLCs, RTUs, DCS, or SCADA controllers, alarm thresholds changed, or unauthorized commands issued to control equipment, which could potentially result in damage to equipment (if tolerances are exceeded), premature shutdown of processes (such as prematurely shutting down transmission lines), causing an environmental incident, or even disabling control equipment

False information sent to control system operators either to disguise unauthorized changes or to initiate inappropriate actions by system operators

Control system software or configuration settings modified, producing unpredictable results

Safety systems operation interfered with

Malicious software (e.g., virus, worm, Trojan horse) introduced into the system

Recipes (i.e., the materials and directions for creating a product) or work instructions modified in order to bring about damage to products, equipment, or personnel

In addition, in control systems that cover a wide geographic area, the remote sites are often not staffed and may not be physically monitored. If such remote systems are physically breached, the adversaries could establish a connection back to the control network.

The following are two hypothetical ICS incident scenarios [11]:

Using war dialers—simple computer programs that dial consecutive phone numbers looking for modems—an adversary finds modems connected to the programmable breakers of the electric power transmission control system, cracks the passwords that control access to the breakers, and changes the control settings to cause local power outages and damage equipment. The adversary lowers the settings from 500 Ampere (A) to 200 A on some circuit breakers, taking those lines out of service and diverting power to neighboring lines. At the same time, the adversary raises the settings on neighboring lines to 900 A, preventing the circuit breakers from tripping, thus overloading the lines. This causes significant damage to transformers and other critical equipment, resulting in lengthy repair outages.

A power plant serving a large metropolitan district has logically isolated the control system from the corporate network of the plant, installed state-of-the-art firewalls, and implemented intrusion detection and prevention technology. An engineer innocently downloads information about a continuing education seminar at a local college, inadvertently introducing a virus into the control network. Just before the morning peak, the operator screens go blank and the system is shut down.

Although these scenarios are hypothetical, they represent potential incident scenarios for an ICS. Section 3.7 provides summaries of several actual ICS incidents.

3.6 Sources of Incidents

An accurate accounting of cyber incidents on control systems is difficult to determine. However, individuals in the industry who have been focusing on this issue see similar growth trends between vulnerabilities exposed in traditional IT systems and those being found in control systems. There is a Repository of Security Incidents (RISI)[3], which is designed to track incidents of a cyber security nature that directly affect ICS and processes. This includes events such as accidental cyber-related incidents, as well as deliberate events such as unauthorized remote access, DoS attacks, and malware infiltrations. Data is collected through research into publicly known incidents and from private reporting by member organizations that wish to have access to the database. Each incident is investigated and then rated according to reliability (confirmed, likely but unconfirmed, unlikely or unknown, and hoax/urban legend).

The data collected includes the following:

Incident title

Date of incident

Reliability of report

Type of incident (e.g., accident, virus)

Industry (e.g., petroleum, automotive)

Entry point (e.g., Internet, wireless, modem)

Perpetrator

Type of system and hardware impacted

Brief description of incident

Impact on organization

Measures to prevent recurrence

References.

As of June 2006, 119 incidents had been investigated and logged in the database, with 15 incidents still pending investigation. Of these, 13 were flagged as hoax or unlikely and removed from the study data. Figure 3-1 shows the trend of incidents between 1982 and 2006, which shows a sharp increase in incidents starting around 2001. The complexity of modern ICS leaves many vulnerabilities as well as vectors for attack. Attacks can come from many places, including indirectly through the corporate network or directly via the Internet, virtual private networks (VPN), wireless networks, and dial-up modems.

---

[3] The Repository of Security Incidents (RISI) can be found at: http://www.securityincidents.org/

Other sources of control system impact information show an increase in control system incidents as well. It is not clear whether there are more incidents happening or just more are being detected and reported.

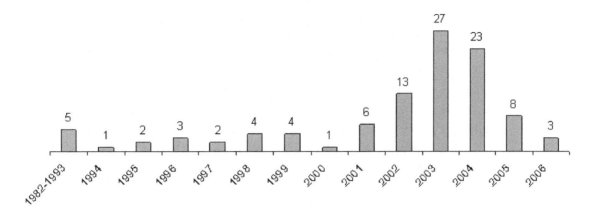

Figure 3-1. Industrial Security Incidents by Year

There are three broad categories of control system incidents:

Intentional targeted attacks such as gaining unauthorized access to files, performing a DoS, or spoofing e-mails (i.e., forging the sender's identity for an e-mail)

Unintentional consequences or collateral damage from worms, viruses or control system failures

Unintentional internal security consequences, such as inappropriate testing of operational systems or unauthorized system configuration changes.

Of the three, targeted attacks are the least frequent. Targeted attacks are potentially the most damaging, but also require detailed knowledge of the system and supporting infrastructure. Therefore, the most likely threat agents are unintentional threats and disgruntled employees, former employees, and others that have worked with or for the organization.[12].

3.7 Documented Incidents

As mentioned in Section 3.6, there are three broad categories of ICS incidents including intentional attacks, unintentional consequences or collateral damage from worms, viruses or control system failures, and unintentional internal security consequences, such as inappropriate testing of operational systems or unauthorized system configuration changes. Reported incidents from these categories include the following:

Intentional Attacks

Worcester Air Traffic Communications[4]. In March 1997, a teenager in Worcester, Massachusetts disabled part of the public switched telephone network using a dial-up modem connected to the system. This knocked out phone service at the control tower, airport security, the airport fire department, the weather service, and carriers that use the airport. Also, the tower's main radio transmitter and another transmitter that activates runway lights were shut down, as well as a printer that controllers use to monitor flight progress. The attack also knocked out phone service to 600 homes and businesses in the nearby town of Rutland.

---

[4] Additional information on the Worcester Air Traffic Communications incident can be found at:
http://www.cnn.com/TECH/computing/9803/18/juvenile.hacker/index.html

Maroochy Shire Sewage Spill[5]. In the spring of 2000, a former employee of an Australian organization that develops manufacturing software applied for a job with the local government, but was rejected. Over a two-month period, the disgruntled rejected employee reportedly used a radio transmitter on as many as 46 occasions to remotely break into the controls of a sewage treatment system. He altered electronic data for particular sewerage pumping stations and caused malfunctions in their operations, ultimately releasing about 264,000 gallons of raw sewage into nearby rivers and parks.

Stuxnet Worm[6]. Stuxnet is a Microsoft Windows computer worm discovered in July 2010 that specifically targets industrial software and equipment. The worm initially spreads indiscriminately, but includes a highly specialized malware payload that is designed to target only specific SCADA systems that are configured to control and monitor specific industrial processes.

Unintentional Consequences

CSX Train Signaling System[7]. In August 2003, the Sobig computer virus was blamed for shutting down train signaling systems throughout the east coast of the U.S. The virus infected the computer system at CSX Corp.'s Jacksonville, Florida headquarters, shutting down signaling, dispatching, and other systems. According to Amtrak spokesman Dan Stessel, ten Amtrak trains were affected in the morning. Trains between Pittsburgh and Florence, South Carolina were halted because of dark signals, and one regional Amtrak train from Richmond, Virginia to Washington and New York was delayed for more than two hours. Long-distance trains were also delayed between four and six hours.

Davis-Besse[8]. In August 2003, the Nuclear Regulatory Commission confirmed that in January 2003, the Microsoft SQL Server worm known as Slammer infected a private computer network at the idled Davis-Besse nuclear power plant in Oak Harbor, Ohio, disabling a safety monitoring system for nearly five hours. In addition, the plant's process computer failed, and it took about six hours for it to become available again. Slammer reportedly also affected communications on the control networks of at least five other utilities by propagating so quickly that control system traffic was blocked.

Northeast Power Blackout[9]. In August 2003, failure of the alarm processor in First Energy's SCADA system prevented control room operators from having adequate *situational awareness* of critical operational changes to the electrical grid. Additionally, effective reliability oversight was prevented when the state estimator at the Midwest Independent System Operator failed due to incomplete information on topology changes, preventing contingency analysis. Several key 345 kV transmission lines in Northern Ohio trip due to contact with trees. This eventually initiates cascading overloads of additional 345 kV and 138 kV lines, leading to an uncontrolled cascading failure of the grid. A total of 61,800 MW load was lost as 508 generating units at 265 power plants tripped.

---

[5]   Additional information on the Maroochy Shire Sewage Spill incident can be found at:
       http://www.theregister.co.uk/2001/10/31/hacker_jailed_for_revenge_sewage/

[6]   Additional information on the Stuxnet worm can be found at: http://en.wikipedia.org/wiki/Stuxnet

[7]   Additional information on the CSX Train Signaling System incident can found at:
       http://www.cbsnews.com/stories/2003/08/21/tech/main569418.shtml and
       http://www.informationweek.com/story/showArticle.jhtml?articleID=13100807

[8]   Additional information on the Davis-Besse incident can found at: http://www.securityfocus.com/news/6767

[9]   Additional information on the Northeast Power Blackout incident can found at:
       http://www.oe.energy.gov/DocumentsandMedia/BlackoutFinal-Web.pdf

Zotob Worm[10]**.** In August 2005, a round of Internet worm infections knocked 13 of DaimlerChrysler's U.S. automobile manufacturing plants offline for almost an hour, stranding workers as infected Microsoft Windows systems were patched. Plants in Illinois, Indiana, Wisconsin, Ohio, Delaware, and Michigan were knocked offline. While the worm affected primarily Windows 2000 systems, it also affected some early versions of Windows XP. Symptoms include the repeated shutdown and rebooting of a computer. Zotob and its variations caused computer outages at heavy-equipment maker Caterpillar Inc., aircraft-maker Boeing, and several large U.S. news organizations.

Taum Sauk Water Storage Dam Failure[11]**.** In December 2005, the Taum Sauk Water Storage Dam suffered a catastrophic failure releasing a billion gallons of water. The failure of the reservoir occurred as the reservoir was being filled to capacity or may have possibly been overtopped. The current working theory is that the reservoir's berm was overtopped when the routine nightly pump-back operation failed to cease when the reservoir was filled. According to AmerenUE, the gauges at the dam read differently than the gauges at the Osage plant at the Lake of the Ozarks, which monitors and operates the Taum Sauk plant remotely. The stations are linked together using a network of microwave towers, and there are no operators on-site at Taum Sauk.

Bellingham, Washington Gasoline Pipeline Failure[12]**.** In June 1999, 900,000 liters (237,000 gallons) of gasoline leaked from a 16" pipeline and ignited 1.5 hours later causing 3 deaths, 8 injuries, and extensive property damage. The pipeline failure was exacerbated by control systems not able to perform control and monitoring functions. "Immediately prior to and during the incident, the SCADA system exhibited poor performance that inhibited the pipeline controllers from seeing and reacting to the development of an abnormal pipeline operation." A key recommendation from the NTSB report issued October 2002 was to utilize an off-line development and testing system for implementing and testing changes to the SCADA database.

[10] Additional information on the Zotob Worm incident can found at: http://www.eweek.com/article2/0,1895,1849914,00.asp and http://www.computerwire.com/industries/research/?pid=750E3094-C77B-4E85-AA27-2C1D26D919C7
[11] Additional information on the Taum Sauk Water Storage Dam Failure incident can found at: http://en.wikipedia.org/wiki/Taum_Sauk_Dam_Failure
[12] Additional information on Bellingham, Washington Gasoline Pipeline Failure incident can found at www.ntsb.gov/publictn/2002/PAR0202.pdf

Unintentional Internal Security Consequences

Vulnerability Scanner Incidents[13]. While a ping sweep was being performed on an active SCADA network that controlled 3 meter (9 foot) robotic arms, it was noticed that one arm became active and swung around 180 degrees. The controller for the arm was in standby mode before the ping sweep was initiated. In a separate incident, a ping sweep was being performed on an ICS network to identify all hosts that were attached to the network, for inventory purposes, and it caused a system controlling the creation of integrated circuits in the fabrication plant to hang. This test resulted in the destruction of $50,000 worth of wafers. See Section 4.2.6 for additional guidance on ICS vulnerability assessments.

Penetration Testing Incident[14]. A natural gas utility hired an IT security consulting organization to conduct penetration testing on its corporate IT network. The consulting organization carelessly ventured into a part of the network that was directly connected to the SCADA system. The penetration test locked up the SCADA system and the utility was not able to send gas through its pipelines for four hours. The outcome was the loss of service to its customer base for those four hours.

---

[13]   Additional information on vulnerability scanner incidents can found at:
http://www.sandia.gov/scada/documents/sand_2005_2846p.pdf

[14]   Additional information on penetration testing incidents can found at:
http://www.sandia.gov/scada/documents/sand_2005_2846p.pdf

4. ICS Security Program Development and Deployment

As described in Section 3.1, there are critical operational differences between ICS and IT systems that influence how specific security controls should be applied to the ICS. Accordingly, organizations should develop and deploy an ICS security program.[15] ICS security plans and programs should be consistent with and integrated with existing IT security experience, programs, and practices, but must be tailored to the specific requirements and characteristics of ICS technologies and environments. Organizations should review and update their ICS security plans and programs regularly to reflect changes in technologies, operations, standards, and regulations, as well as the security needs of specific facilities.

This section provides an overview of the development and deployment of an ICS security program. Section 4.1 describes how to establish a business case for an ICS security program, including suggested content for the business case. Section 4.2 discusses the development of a comprehensive ICS security program and provides information on several major steps in deploying the program. Information on specific security controls that might be implemented as part of the security program is given in Sections 5 and 6 of the document.

4.1 Business Case for Security

The first step in implementing a cyber security program for ICS is to develop a compelling business case for the unique needs of the organization. The business case should capture the business concerns of senior management while being founded in the experience of those who are already dealing with many of the same risks. The business case provides the business impact and financial justification for creating an integrated cyber security program. It should include detailed information about the following:

Benefits, including improved control system reliability and availability, of creating an integrated security program

Prioritized potential costs and damage scenarios if a cyber security program for the ICS is not implemented

High-level overview of the process required to implement, operate, monitor, review, maintain, and improve the cyber security program

Costs and resources required to develop, implement and maintain the security program.

Before presenting the business case to management, there should be a well-thought-out and developed security implementation and cost plan. For example, simply requesting a firewall is insufficient for numerous reasons.

4.1.1 Benefits

Responsible risk management policy mandates that the threat to the ICS should be measured and monitored to protect the interests of employees, the public, shareholders, customers, vendors, and society. Risk analysis enables costs and benefits to be weighed so that informed decisions can be made on protective actions. In addition to reducing risks, exercising due-diligence and displaying responsibility also helps organizations by:

Improving control system reliability and availability

---

[15] The Instrumentation, Systems, and Automation (ISA) 99 Committee http://www.isa.org/isa99 has developed ANSI/ISA-99.02.01-2009, a standard that addresses the development and deployment of an ICS security program in detail.

Improving employee morale, loyalty, and retention

Reducing community concerns

Increasing investor confidence

Reducing legal liabilities

Enhancing the corporate image and reputation

Helping with insurance coverage and cost

Improving investor and banking relations.

A strong safety and cyber security management program is fundamental to a sustainable business model.

4.1.2 Potential Consequences

The importance of secure systems should be further emphasized as business reliance on interconnectivity increases. DoS attacks and malware (e.g., worms, viruses) have become all too common and have already impacted ICS. In addition, a cyber breach in some critical infrastructures can have significant physical impacts. The major categories of impacts are as follows:

Physical Impacts. Physical impacts encompass the set of direct consequences of ICS failure. The potential effects of paramount importance include personal injury and loss of life. Other effects include the loss of property (including data) and potential damage to the environment.

Economic Impacts. Economic impacts are a second-order effect from physical impacts ensuing from an ICS incident. Physical impacts could result in repercussions to system operations, which in turn inflict a greater economic loss on the facility or organization. On a larger scale, these effects could negatively impact the local, regional, national, or possibly global economy.

Social Impacts. Another second-order effect, the consequence from the loss of national or public confidence in an organization, is many times overlooked. It is, however, a very real target and one that could be accomplished through an ICS incident.

Potential consequences of an ICS incident are listed below. Note that items in this list are not independent. In fact, one can lead to another. For example, release of hazardous material can lead to injury or death.

Impact on national security—facilitate an act of terrorism

Reduction or loss of production at one site or multiple sites simultaneously

Injury or death of employees

Injury or death of persons in the community

Damage to equipment

Release, diversion, or theft of hazardous materials

Environmental damage

Violation of regulatory requirements

Product contamination

Criminal or civil legal liabilities

Loss of proprietary or confidential information

Loss of brand image or customer confidence.

Undesirable incidents of any sort detract from the value of an organization, but safety and security incidents can have longer-term negative impacts than other types of incidents on all stakeholders—employees, shareholders, customers, and the communities in which an organization operates.

4.1.3 Key Components of the Business Case

There are four key components of the business case: prioritized threats, prioritized business consequences, prioritized business benefits, and estimated annual business impact.

4.1.3.1 Prioritized Threats

The list of potential threats provided in Section 3.2 needs to be refined to those threats that the organization believes could reasonably impact the facility to be secured. For instance, a food and beverage organization might not find terrorism a credible threat but might be more concerned with viruses, worms, and disgruntled employees.

4.1.3.2 Prioritized Business Consequences

The list of potential business consequences provided in Section 4.1.2 needs to be distilled to the particular business consequences that senior management will find the most compelling. For instance, a food and beverage organization that handles no toxic or flammable materials and typically processes its product at relatively low temperatures and pressures might not be concerned about equipment damage or environmental impact, but might be more concerned about loss of production availability and degradation of product quality. Regulatory compliance might also be a concern. Individuals should not minimize the potential consequences to avoid taking proper security risk mitigation actions.

The Sarbanes-Oxley Act requires corporate leaders to sign off on compliance with information accuracy and protection of corporate information.[16] Also, the demonstration of due diligence is required by most internal and external audit firms to satisfy shareholders and other organization stakeholders. By implementing a comprehensive cyber security program, management is exercising due diligence.

4.1.3.3 Prioritized Business Benefits

Improved control systems security and control system specific security policies can potentially improve control system reliability and availability. This also includes minimizing unintentional control system cyber security impacts from inappropriate testing, policies, and misconfigured systems.

4.1.3.4 Estimated Annual Business Impact

The highest priority items shown in the list of prioritized business consequences should be evaluated to obtain an estimate of the annual business impact, preferably but not necessarily in financial terms. For the food and beverage organization example, the organization may have experienced a virus incident within its internal network that the information security staff estimated as resulting in a specific financial

---

[16] More information on the act, and a copy of the act itself, can be found at http://www.sec.gov/about/laws.shtml.

cost. If the internal network and the control network are interconnected, it is conceivable that a virus originating from the control network could cause the same amount of business impact. NIST SP 800-39 [19] and ISO/IEC 27002 provide additional guidance on business impact.

4.1.4 Resources for Building Business Case

The main resources for information to help form a business case are external resources in trade and standards organizations, consulting firms and internal resources in related risk management programs or engineering and operations. External resources in trade and standards organizations can often provide useful tips as to what factors most strongly influenced their management to support their efforts and what resources within their organizations proved most helpful. For different industries, these factors may be different, but there may be similarities in the roles that other risk management specialists can play. Appendix C provides a list and short description of some of the current activities in ICS security.

Internal resources in related risk management efforts (e.g., information security, health, safety and environmental risk, physical security, business continuity) can provide tremendous assistance based on their experience with related incidents in the organization. This information is helpful from the standpoint of prioritizing threats and estimating business impact. These resources can also provide insight into which managers are focused on dealing with which risks and, thus, which managers might be the most appropriate or receptive to serving as a champion. Internal resources in control systems engineering and operations can provide insight into the details of how control systems are deployed within the organization, such as the following:

How networks are typically segregated

What remote access connections are generally employed

How high-risk control systems or safety instrumented systems are typically designed

What security countermeasures are commonly used

4.1.5 Presenting the Business Case to Leadership

The business leadership will be responsible for approving and driving cyber security policies, assigning security roles, and implementing the cyber security program across the organization. Funding for the entire program can usually be done in phases. While some funding may be required to start the cyber security activity, additional funding can be obtained later as the security vulnerabilities and needs of the program are better understood and additional strategies are developed. Additionally, the costs (both direct and indirect) should be considered for retrofitting the ICS for security vs. addressing security to begin with.

Often, a good approach to obtain management buy-in to address the problem is to ground the business case in a successful actual third-party example. The business case should present to management that the other organization had the same problem and then present that they found a solution and how they solved it. This will often prompt management to ask what the solution is and how it might be applicable to their organization.

4.2 Developing a Comprehensive Security Program

Effectively integrating security into an ICS requires defining and executing a comprehensive program that addresses all aspects of security, ranging from identifying objectives to day-to-day operation and ongoing auditing for compliance and improvement. This section describes the basic process for developing a security program, including the following:

Obtain senior management buy-in

Build and train a cross-functional team

Define charter and scope

Define specific ICS policies and procedures

Define and inventory ICS assets

Perform a risk and vulnerability assessment

Define the mitigation controls

Provide training and raise security awareness for ICS staff.

More detailed information on the various steps is provided in ANSI/ISA-99.02.01 *Security for Industrial Automation and Control Systems: Establishing an Industrial Automation and Control Systems Security Program.*

The commitment to a security program begins at the top. Senior management must demonstrate a clear commitment to cyber security. Cyber security is a business responsibility shared by all members of the enterprise and especially by leading members of the business, process, and management teams. Cyber security programs with adequate funding and visible, top-level support from organization leaders are more likely to achieve compliance, function more smoothly, and have greater success than programs that do not have that support.

Whenever a new system is being designed and installed, it is imperative to take the time to address security throughout the lifecycle, from architecture to procurement to installation to maintenance to decommissioning. There are serious risks in deploying systems to production based on the assumption that they will be secured later. If there is insufficient time and resources to secure the system properly before deployment, it is unlikely that there will be sufficient time and resources later to address security.

4.2.1   Senior Management Buy-in

It is critical for the success of the ICS security program that senior management [29] buy into and participate in the ICS security program. Senior management needs to be at a level that encompasses both IT and ICS operations.

4.2.2   Build and Train a Cross-Functional Team

It is essential for a cross-functional cyber security team to share their varied domain knowledge and experience to evaluate and mitigate risk in the ICS. At a minimum, the cyber security team should consist of a member of the organization's IT staff, a control engineer, a control system operator, security subject matter experts, and a member of the management staff. Security knowledge and skills should include network architecture and design, security processes and practices, and secure infrastructure design and operation. For continuity and completeness, the cyber security team should also include the control system vendor and/or system integrator. The cyber security team should report directly to site management (e.g., facility superintendent) or the company's CIO/CSO, who in turn, accepts complete responsibility and accountability for the cyber security of the ICS. Management level accountability will help ensure an ongoing commitment to cyber security efforts.

While the control engineers will play a large role in securing the ICS, they will not be able to do so without collaboration and support from both the IT department and management. IT often has years of security experience, much of which is applicable to ICS. As the cultures of control engineering and IT are often significantly different and unknown to the other party, significant cross-cultural understanding and integration will be essential for the development of a collaborative security design and operation.

4.2.3   Define Charter and Scope

The cyber security team should establish the corporate policy that defines the guiding charter of the security organization and the roles, responsibilities, and accountabilities of system owners and users. The team should decide upon and document the objective of the security program, the business organizations affected, all the computer systems and networks involved, the budget and resources required, and the division of responsibilities. The scope can also address business, training, audit, legal, and regulatory requirements, as well as timetables and responsibilities.

There may already be a program in place or being developed for the organization's IT business systems. The team should identify which existing practices to leverage and which practices are specific to the control system. In the long run, it will be easier to get positive results if the team can share resources with others in the organization that have similar objectives.

4.2.4   Define ICS Specific Security Policies and Procedures

Policies and procedures are at the root of every successful security program and wherever possible, ICS specific security polices and procedures should be integrated with existing operational/management policies. The more transparent these policies are with all other procedures, the more likely they will be implemented at all levels. Policies and procedures help to ensure that security protection is both consistent and current to protect against evolving threats, and also help to educate. After the risks for the various systems are clearly understood, the cyber security team should examine existing security policies to see if they adequately address the risks to the ICS. If needed, existing policies should be revised or new policies created to address desktop and business systems as well as the ICS. Few organizations have the resources to harden the ICS against all possible threats; management should guide the development of the security policies, based on a risk assessment that will set the security priorities and goals for the organization so that the risks posed by the threats are mitigated sufficiently. Procedures that support the policies need to be developed so that the policies are implemented fully and properly for the ICS. Security procedures should be documented, tested, and updated periodically in response to policy and technology changes. Consider developing ICS security policies and procedures based on the Homeland Security Advisory System Threat Level, deploying increasingly heightened security postures as the Threat Level increases.

4.2.5   Define and Inventory ICS Systems and Networks Assets

The cyber security team should identify the applications and computer systems within the ICS, as well as the networks within and interfacing to the ICS. The focus should be on systems rather than just devices, and should include PLCs, DCS, SCADA, and instrument-based systems that use a monitoring device such as an HMI. Assets that use a routable protocol or are dial-up accessible should be documented. As the team identifies the ICS assets, the information should be recorded in a standard format. The team should review and update the ICS asset list annually.

There are several commercial enterprise inventory tools that can identify and document all hardware and software resident on a network. Care must be taken before using these tools to identify ICS assets; teams should first conduct an assessment of how these tools work and what impact they might have on the connected control equipment. Tool evaluation may include testing in similar, non-production control system environments to ensure that the tools do not adversely impact the production systems. Impact could be due to the nature of the information or the volume of network traffic. While this impact may be acceptable in IT systems, it is not acceptable in an ICS. Additional information and guidance on scanning and inventory tools is provided in Section 4.2.6.

4.2.6   Perform Risk and Vulnerability Assessment

Because every organization has a limited set of resources, organizations should perform a risk assessment for the ICS systems and use its results to prioritize the ICS systems based on the potential impact to each system. The organization should then perform a detailed vulnerability assessment for the highest-priority systems and assessments for lower-priority systems as deemed prudent/as resources allow. The vulnerability assessment will help identify any weaknesses that may be present in the systems that could allow the confidentiality, integrity, or availability of systems and data to be adversely affected, along with the related cyber security risks and mitigation approaches to reduce the risks.

Because of the potential for disruption to the devices, vulnerability scanners should be used with caution on production ICS networks [30]. A major concern is an accidental DoS to devices and networks. Vulnerability scanners often attempt to verify vulnerabilities by extensively probing and conducting a representative set of attacks against devices and networks. ICS were designed and built to control and automate real-world processes or equipment. Given the wrong instructions, they could perform incorrect actions, causing product loss, equipment damage, injury, or even deaths.

The following examples [31] demonstrate the danger:

> While a ping sweep was being performed on an active SCADA network that controlled 9-foot robotic arms, it was noticed that one arm became active and swung around 180 degrees. The controller for the arm was in standby mode before the ping sweep was initiated.

> On an ICS network, a ping sweep was being performed to identify all hosts that were attached to the network, for inventory purposes, and it caused a system controlling the creation of integrated circuits in the fabrication plant to lock-up. This test resulted in the destruction of $50,000 worth of wafers.

> A natural gas utility hired an IT security consulting organization to conduct penetration testing on its corporate IT network. The consulting organization carelessly ventured into a part of the network that was directly connected to the SCADA system. The penetration test locked up the SCADA system and the utility was not able to send gas through its pipelines for four hours. The outcome was the loss of service to its customer base for those four hours.

Identifying the vulnerabilities within an ICS requires a different approach from that of a typical IT system. In most cases, devices on an IT system can be rebooted, restored, or replaced with little interruption of service to its customers. An ICS controls a physical process and therefore has real-world consequences associated with its actions. Some actions are time-critical, while others have a more relaxed timeframe.

When performing an inventory or vulnerability scan on a system or network segment, there are several steps that are generally performed. Each step is listed in Table 4-1, along with the usual IT action and alternate suggested actions that should be taken instead for an ICS, making the outcomes of any testing safer. These techniques may make the work somewhat more difficult, but should help to mitigate problems associated with active scanning.

Table 4-1. Suggested Actions for ICS Vulnerability Assessments

To Be Identified	Usual IT Action	Suggested ICS Actions
Hosts, nodes, and networks	Ping sweep (e.g., nmap)	• Examine router configuration files or route tables • Perform physical verification (chasing wires) • Conduct passive network listening or use intrusion detection (e.g., snort) on the network • Specify a subset of IP addresses to be programmatically scanned
Services	Port scan (e.g., nmap)	• Do local port verification (e.g., netstat) • Scan a duplicate, development, or test system on a non-production network
Vulnerabilities within a service	Vulnerability scan (e.g., nessus)	• Perform local banner grabbing with version lookup in Common Vulnerabilities and Exposures (CVE) • Scan a duplicate, development, or test system on a non-production network

The commonality among the suggested ICS actions is that they do not generate traffic on production operational networks or against production systems. These less intrusive methods can gather most, if not all, of the same information as more active methods, without the risk of causing a failure during testing. Another factor to consider when choosing ICS testing methods is that these systems have little spare capacity as compared to IT systems. ICS systems have much greater longevity than their IT counterparts, so their hardware is often well behind the state-of-the-art and can be easily overtaxed. Also, ICS systems usually run at slow speeds on legacy networks that can be overwhelmed by the volume of traffic generated during active testing.

When any assessment of an ICS is being performed, ICS personnel must be aware that testing is occurring, and be prepared to immediately address any problems that arise. If manual control of the system is possible, personnel capable of performing manual control should be present during the security testing. Additionally, security auditors need to understand the ICS under test, the risk involved with the test, and the consequences associated with unintentional stimulus or DoS to the ICS.

4.2.7 Define the Mitigation Controls

Organizations should analyze the detailed risk assessment, identify the cost of mitigation for each risk, compare the cost with the risk of occurrence, and select those mitigation controls where cost is less than the potential risk. Because it is usually impractical or impossible to eliminate all risks, organizations should focus on mitigating risk with the greatest potential impact to the ICS and the process.

The controls to mitigate a specific risk may vary among types of systems. For example, user authentication controls might be different for ICS than for corporate payroll systems and e-commerce systems. Organizations should document and communicate the selected controls, along with the procedures for using the controls. As the team identifies mitigation strategies, risks may be identified that can be mitigated by "quick fix" solutions—low-cost, high-value practices that can significantly reduce risk. Examples of these solutions are restricting Internet access and eliminating e-mail access on operator control stations or consoles. Organizations should identify, evaluate, and implement suitable quick fix solutions as soon as possible to reduce security risks and achieve rapid benefits. The Department of

Energy (DOE) has a "21 Steps to Improve Cyber Security of SCADA Networks" [32] document that could be used as a starting point to outline specific actions to increase the security of SCADA systems and other ICS.

4.2.8 Provide Training and Raise Security Awareness

Security awareness is a critical part of ICS incident prevention, particularly when it comes to social engineering threats. Social engineering is a technique used to manipulate individuals into giving away private information, such as passwords. This information can then be used to compromise otherwise secure systems.

Implementing an ICS security program may bring changes to the way in which personnel access computer programs, applications, and the computer desktop itself. Organizations should design effective training and awareness programs and communication vehicles to help employees understand why new access and control methods are required, ideas they can use to reduce risks, and the impact on the organization if control methods are not incorporated. Training programs also demonstrate management's commitment to, and the value of, a cyber security program. Feedback from staff exposed to this type of training can be a valuable source of input for refining the charter and scope of the security program.

5. Network Architecture

When designing a network architecture for an ICS deployment, it is usually recommended to separate the ICS network from the corporate network. The nature of network traffic on these two networks is different: Internet access, FTP, e-mail, and remote access will typically be permitted on the corporate network but should not be allowed on the ICS network. Rigorous change control procedures for network equipment, configuration, and software changes may not be in place on the corporate network. If ICS network traffic is carried on the corporate network, it could be intercepted or be subjected to a DoS attack. By having separate networks, security and performance problems on the corporate network should not be able to affect the ICS network.

Practical considerations often mean that a connection is required between the ICS and corporate networks. This connection is a significant security risk and careful consideration should be given to the design and implementation. If the networks must be connected, it is strongly recommended that only minimal (single if possible) connections be allowed and that the connection is through a firewall and a DMZ. A DMZ is a separate network segment that connects directly to the firewall. Servers containing the data from the ICS that needs to be accessed from the corporate network are put on this network segment. Only these systems should be accessible from the corporate network. With any external connections, the minimum access should be permitted through the firewall, including opening only the ports required for specific communication. The following sections describe the access required for specific node types.

5.1 Firewalls

Network firewalls are devices or systems that control the flow of network traffic between networks employing differing security postures. In most modern applications, firewalls and firewall environments are discussed in the context of Internet connectivity and the TCP/IP protocol suite. However, firewalls have applicability in network environments that do not include or require Internet connectivity. For example, many corporate networks employ firewalls to restrict connectivity to and from internal networks servicing more sensitive functions, such as the accounting or human resource departments. By employing firewalls to control connectivity to these areas, an organization can prevent unauthorized access to the respective systems and resources within the more sensitive areas. There are three general classes of firewalls:

Packet Filtering Firewalls. The most basic type of firewall is called a packet filter. Packet filter firewalls are essentially routing devices that include access control functionality for system addresses and communication sessions. The access control is governed by a set of directives collectively referred to as a rule set. In their most basic form, packet filters operate at layer 3 (network) of the Open Systems Interconnection (OSI) model. This type of firewall checks basic information in each packet, such as IP addresses, against a set of criteria before forwarding the packet. Depending on the packet and the criteria, the firewall can drop the packet, forward it, or send a message to the originator. The advantages of packet filtering firewalls include low cost and low impact on network performance, usually because only one or a few header fields in the packet are examined.

Stateful Inspection Firewalls. Stateful inspection firewalls are packet filters that incorporate added awareness of the OSI model data at layer 4. Stateful inspection firewalls filter packets at the network layer, determine whether session packets are legitimate, and evaluate the contents of packets at the transport layer (e.g., TCP, UDP) as well. Stateful inspection keeps track of active sessions and uses that information to determine if packets should be forwarded or blocked. It offers a high level of security and good performance, but it may be more expensive and complex to administer. Additional rule sets for ICS applications may be required.

Application-Proxy Gateway Firewalls. This class of firewalls examines packets at the application layer and filters traffic based on specific application rules, such as specified applications (e.g., browsers) or protocols (e.g., FTP). It offers a high level of security, but could have overhead and delay impacts on network performance, which can be unacceptable in an ICS environment.

NIST SP 800-41, *Guidelines on Firewalls and Firewall Policy*, provides general guidance for the selection of firewalls and the firewall policies.

In an ICS environment, firewalls are most often deployed between the ICS network and the corporate network [33]. Properly configured, they can greatly restrict undesired access to and from control system host computers and controllers, thereby improving security. They can also potentially improve a control network's responsiveness by removing non-essential traffic from the network. When properly designed, configured, and maintained, dedicated hardware firewalls can contribute significantly to increasing the security of today's ICS environments.

Firewalls provide several tools to enforce a security policy that cannot be accomplished locally on the current set of process control devices available in the market, including the ability to:

Block all communications with the exception of specifically enabled communications between devices on the unprotected LAN and protected ICS networks. Blocking is based on source and destination IP address pairs, services, and ports. Blocking can occur on both inbound and outbound packets, which is helpful in limiting high-risk communications such as e-mail.

Enforce secure authentication of all users seeking to gain access to the ICS network. There is flexibility to employ varying protection levels of authentication methods including simple passwords, complex passwords, multi-factor authentication technologies, tokens, biometrics and smart cards. Select the particular method based upon the vulnerability of the ICS network to be protected, rather than using the method that is available at the device level.

Enforce destination authorization. Users can be restricted and allowed to reach only the nodes on the control network necessary for their job function. This reduces the potential of users intentionally or accidentally gaining access to and control of devices for which they are not authorized, but adds to the complexity for on-the-job-training or cross-training employees.

Record information flow for traffic monitoring, analysis, and intrusion detection.

Permit the ICS to implement operational policies appropriate to the ICS but that might not be appropriate in an IT network, such as prohibition of less secure communications like email, and permitted use of easy-to-remember usernames and group passwords.

Be designed with documented and minimal (single if possible) connections that permit the ICS network to be severed from the corporate network, should that decision be made, in times of serious cyber incidents.

Other possible deployments include using either host-based firewalls or small standalone hardware firewalls in front of, or running on, individual control devices. Using firewalls on an individual device basis can create significant management overhead, especially in change management of firewall configurations.

There are several issues that must be addressed when deploying firewalls in ICS environments, particularly the following:

The possible addition of delay to control system communications

The lack of experience in the design of rule sets suitable for industrial applications. Firewalls used to protect control systems should be configured so they do not permit either incoming or outgoing traffic by default. The default configuration should only be modified when it is necessary to permit connections to or from trusted systems.

Hardware firewalls require ongoing support, maintenance, and backup. Rule sets need to be reviewed to make sure that they are providing adequate protection in light of ever-changing security threats. System capabilities (e.g., storage space for firewall logs) should be monitored to make sure that the firewall is performing its data collection tasks and can be depended upon in the event of a security violation. Real-time monitoring of firewalls and other security sensors is required to rapidly detect and initiate response to cyber incidents.

5.2   Logically Separated Control Network

The ICS network should, at a minimum, be logically separated from the corporate network on physically separate network devices. When enterprise connectivity is required:

There should be documented and minimal (single if possible) access points between the ICS network and the corporate network. Redundant (i.e., backup) access points, if present, must be documented.

A stateful firewall between the ICS network and corporate network should be configured to deny all traffic except that which is explicitly authorized.

The firewall rules should at a minimum provide source and destination filtering (i.e., filter on media access control [MAC] address), in addition to TCP and User Datagram Protocol (UDP) port filtering and Internet Control Message Protocol (ICMP) type and code filtering.

An acceptable approach to enabling communication between an ICS network and a corporate network is to implement an intermediate DMZ network. The DMZ should be connected to the firewall such that specific (restricted) communication may occur between only the corporate network and the DMZ, and the ICS network and the DMZ. The corporate network and the ICS network should not communicate directly with each other. This approach is described in Sections 5.3.4 and 5.3.5. Additional security may be obtained by implementing a Virtual Private Network (VPN) between the ICS and external networks. Sections 5.8.2 and 6.3.4.2 provide additional information on the use of VPNs.

5.3   Network Segregation

ICS networks and corporate networks can be segregated to enhance cyber security using different architectures. This section describes several possible architectures and explains the advantages and disadvantages of each. Please note that the intent of the diagrams in Section 5.3 is to show the placement of firewalls to segregate the network. Not all devices that would be typically found on the control network or corporate network are shown. Section 5.4 provides guidance on a recommended defense-in-depth architecture.

5.3.1   Dual-Homed Computer/Dual Network Interface Cards (NIC)

Dual-homed computers can pass network traffic from one network to another. A computer without proper security controls could pose additional threats. To prevent this, no systems other than firewalls should be configured as dual-homed to span both the control and corporate networks. All connections between the control network and the corporate network should be through a firewall.

5.3.2 Firewall between Corporate Network and Control Network

By introducing a simple two-port firewall between the corporate and control networks, as shown in Figure 5-1, a significant security improvement can be achieved. Properly configured, a firewall significantly reduces the chance of a successful external attack on the control network.

Unfortunately, two issues still remain with this design. First, if the data historian resides on the corporate network, the firewall must allow the data historian to communicate with the control devices on the control network. A packet originating from a malicious or incorrectly configured host on the corporate network (appearing to be the data historian) would be forwarded to individual PLCs/DCS.

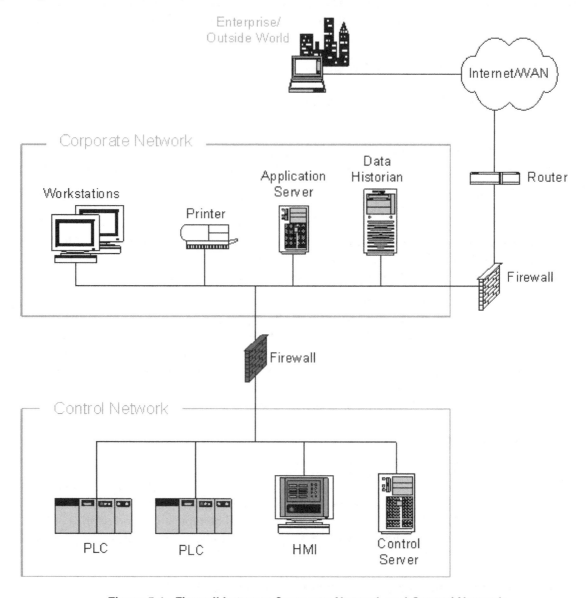

Figure 5-1. Firewall between Corporate Network and Control Network

If the data historian resides on the control network, a firewall rule must exist that allows all hosts from the enterprise to communicate with the historian. Typically, this communication occurs at the application layer as Structured Query Language (SQL) or Hypertext Transfer Protocol (HTTP) requests. Flaws in the historian's application layer code could result in a compromised historian. Once the historian is compromised, the remaining nodes on the control network are vulnerable to a worm propagating or an interactive attack.

Another issue with having a simple firewall between the networks is that spoofed packets can be constructed that can affect the control network, potentially permitting covert data to be tunneled in allowed protocols. For example, if HTTP packets are allowed through the firewall, then Trojan horse software accidentally introduced on an HMI or control network laptop could be controlled by a remote entity and send data (such as captured passwords) to that entity, disguised as legitimate traffic.

In summary, while this architecture is a significant improvement over a non-segregated network, it requires the use of firewall rules that allow direct communications between the corporate network and control network devices. This can result in possible security breaches if not very carefully designed and monitored [34].

5.3.3 Firewall and Router between Corporate Network and Control Network

A slightly more sophisticated design, shown in Figure 5-2, is the use of a router/firewall combination. The router sits in front of the firewall and offers basic packet filtering services, while the firewall handles the more complex issues using either stateful inspection or proxy techniques. This type of design is very popular in Internet-facing firewalls because it allows the faster router to handle the bulk of the incoming packets, especially in the case of DoS attacks, and reduces the load on the firewall. It also offers improved defense-in-depth because there are two different devices an adversary must bypass [34].

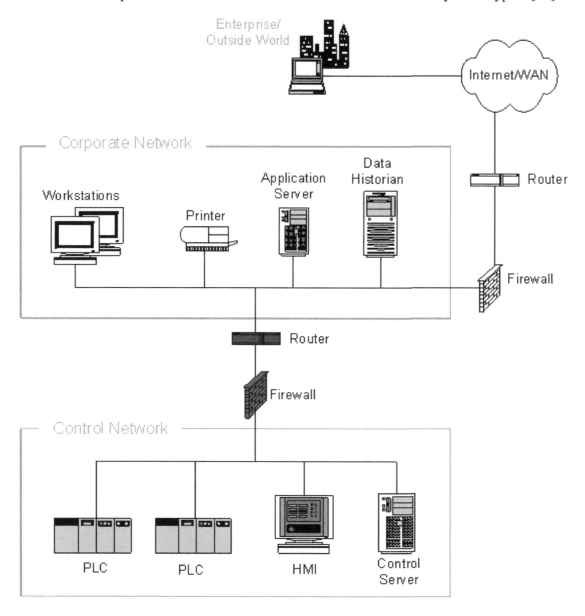

Figure 5-2. Firewall and Router between Corporate Network and Control Network

5.3.4   Firewall with DMZ between Corporate Network and Control Network

A significant improvement is the use of firewalls with the ability to establish a DMZ between the corporate and control networks. Each DMZ holds one or more critical components, such as the data historian, the wireless access point, or remote and third party access systems. In effect, the use of a DMZ-capable firewall allows the creation of an intermediate network.

Creating a DMZ requires that the firewall offer three or more interfaces, rather than the typical public and private interfaces. One of the interfaces is connected to the corporate network, the second to the control network, and the remaining interfaces to the shared or insecure devices such as the data historian server or wireless access points on the DMZ network. Figure 5-3 provides an example of this architecture.

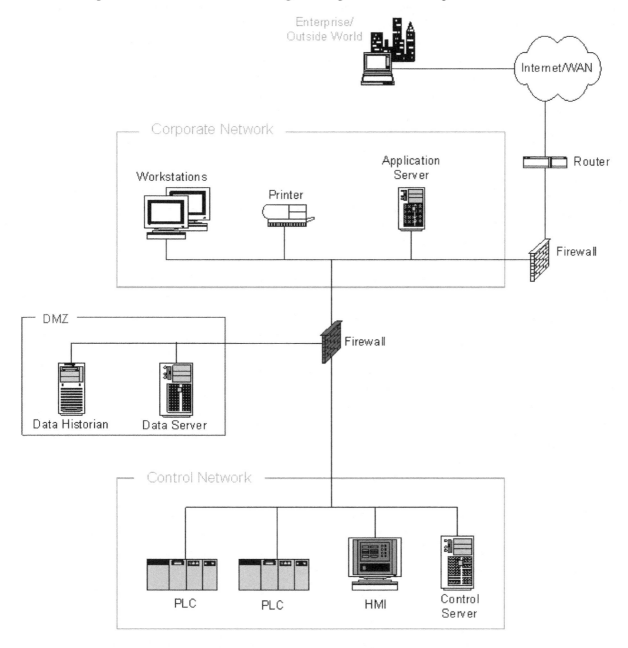

Figure 5-3. Firewall with DMZ between Corporate Network and Control Network

By placing corporate-accessible components in the DMZ, no direct communication paths are required from the corporate network to the control network; each path effectively ends in the DMZ. Most firewalls can allow for multiple DMZs, and can specify what type of traffic may be forwarded between zones. As Figure 5-3 shows, the firewall can block arbitrary packets from the corporate network from entering the control network, and can also regulate traffic from the other network zones including the control network. With well-planned rule sets, a clear separation can be maintained between the control network and other networks, with little or no traffic passing directly between the corporate and control networks.

If a patch management server, an antivirus server, or other security server is to be used for the control network, it should be located directly on the DMZ. Both functions could reside on a single server. Having patch management and antivirus management dedicated to the control network allows for controlled and secure updates that can be tailored for the unique needs of the ICS environment. It may also be helpful if the antivirus product chosen for ICS protection is not the same as the antivirus product used for the corporate network. For example, if a malware incident occurs and one antivirus product cannot detect or stop the malware, it is somewhat likely that another product may have that capability.

The primary security risk in this type of architecture is that if a computer in the DMZ is compromised, then it can be used to launch an attack against the control network via application traffic permitted from the DMZ to the control network. This risk can be greatly reduced if a concerted effort is made to harden and actively patch the servers in the DMZ and if the firewall rule set permits only connections between the control network and DMZ that are initiated by control network devices. Other concerns with this architecture are the added complexity and the potential increased cost of firewalls with several ports. For more critical systems, however, the improved security should more than offset these disadvantages [34].

5.3.5 Paired Firewalls between Corporate Network and Control Network

A variation on the firewall with DMZ solution is to use a pair of firewalls positioned between the corporate and ICS networks, as shown in Figure 5-4. Common servers such as the data historian are situated between the firewalls in a DMZ-like network zone sometimes referred to as a Manufacturing Execution System (MES) layer. As in the architectures described previously, the first firewall blocks arbitrary packets from proceeding to the control network or the shared historians. The second firewall can prevent unwanted traffic from a compromised server from entering the control network, and prevent control network traffic from impacting the shared servers.

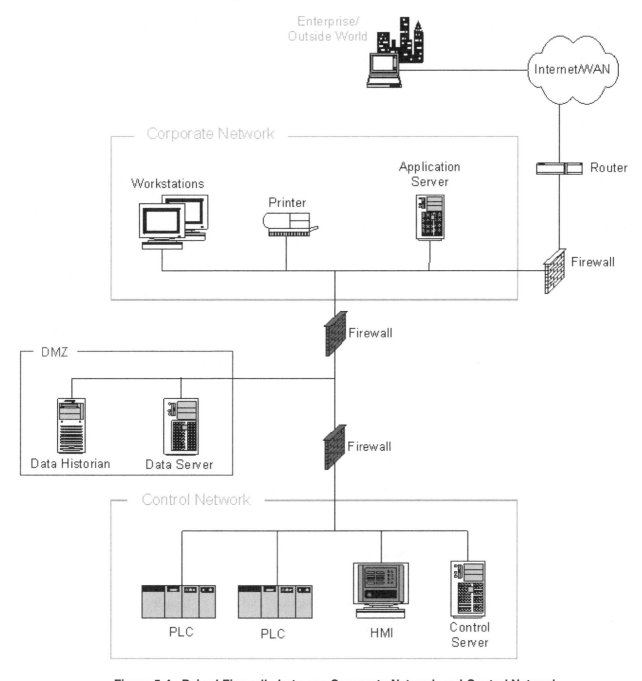

Figure 5-4. Paired Firewalls between Corporate Network and Control Network

If firewalls from two different manufacturers are used, then this solution may offer an advantage. It also allows the control group and the IT group to have clearly separated device responsibility because each can manage a firewall on its own, if the decision is made within the organization to do so. The primary disadvantage with two-firewall architectures is the increased cost and management complexity. For environments with stringent security requirements or the need for clear management separation, this architecture has some strong advantages.

5.3.6 Network Segregation Summary

In summary, non-firewall-based solutions will generally not provide suitable isolation between control networks and corporate networks. The two-zone solutions (no DMZ) are marginally acceptable but should only be deployed with extreme care. The most secure, manageable, and scalable control network and corporate network segregation architectures are typically based on a system with at least three zones, incorporating one or more DMZs.

5.4 Recommended Defense-in-Depth Architecture

A single security product, technology or solution cannot adequately protect an ICS by itself. A multiple layer strategy involving two (or more) different overlapping security mechanisms, a technique also known as defense-in-depth, is desired so that the impact of a failure in any one mechanism is minimized. A defense-in-depth architecture strategy includes the use of firewalls, the creation of demilitarized zones, intrusion detection capabilities along with effective security policies, training programs and incident response mechanisms. In addition, an effective defense-in-depth strategy requires a thorough understanding of possible attack vectors on an ICS. These include:

Backdoors and holes in network perimeter

Vulnerabilities in common protocols

Attacks on field devices

Database attacks

Communications hijacking and 'man-in-the-middle' attacks

Figure 5-5 shows an ICS defense-in-depth architecture strategy that has been developed by the DHS Control Systems Security Program (CSSP) Recommended Practices committee[17] as described in the *Control Systems Cyber Security: Defense in Depth Strategies* [35] document. Additional supporting documents that cover specific issues and associated mitigations are also included on the site. This site will continue to evolve and grow as new recommended practices and related information are added.

The *Control Systems Cyber Security: Defense in Depth Strategies* document provides guidance and direction for developing defense-in-depth architecture strategies for organizations that use control system networks while maintaining a multi-tier information architecture that requires:

Maintenance of various field devices, telemetry collection, and/or industrial-level process systems

Access to facilities via remote data link or modem

Public facing services for customer or corporate operations

---

[17] Information on the CSSP Recommended Practices is located at http://www.us-cert.gov/control_systems/practices/

5-10

This strategy includes firewalls, the use of demilitarized zones and intrusion detection capabilities throughout the ICS architecture. The use of several demilitarized zones in Figure 5-5 provides the added capability to separate functionalities and access privileges and has proved to be very effective in protecting large architectures comprised of networks with different operational mandates. Intrusion detection deployments apply different rule-sets and signatures unique to each domain being monitored.

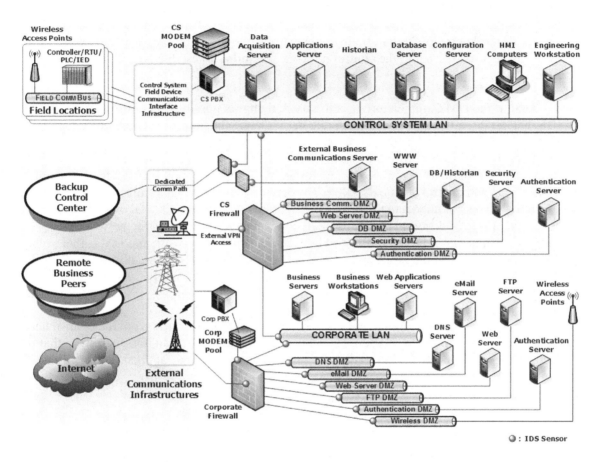

Figure 5-5. CSSP Recommended Defense-In-Depth Architecture

5.5   General Firewall Policies for ICS

Once the defense-in-depth architecture is in place, the work of determining exactly what traffic should be allowed through the firewalls begins. Configuring the firewalls to deny all except for the traffic absolutely required for business needs is every organization's basic premise, but the reality is much more difficult. Exactly what does "absolutely required for business" mean and what are the security impacts of allowing that traffic through? For example, many organizations considered allowing SQL traffic through the firewall as required for business for many data historian servers. Unfortunately, SQL was also the vector for the Slammer worm. Many important protocols used in the industrial world, such as HTTP, FTP, OPC/DCOM, EtherNet/IP, and MODBUS/TCP, have significant security vulnerabilities.

The remaining material in this section summarizes some of the key points from the CPNI *Good Practice Guide on Firewall Deployment for SCADA and Process Control Networks* [34] document.

When installing a single two-port firewall without a DMZ for shared servers (i.e., the architecture described in Section 5.3.2), particular care needs to be taken with the rule design. At a minimum, all rules should be stateful rules that are both IP address and port (application) specific. The address portion of the rules should restrict incoming traffic to a very small set of shared devices (e.g., the data historian) on the control network from a controlled set of addresses on the corporate network. Allowing any IP addresses on the corporate network to access servers inside the control network is not recommended. In addition, the allowed ports should be carefully restricted to relatively secure protocols such as Hypertext Transfer Protocol Secure (HTTPS). Allowing HTTP, FTP, or other unsecured protocols to cross the firewall is a security risk due to the potential for traffic sniffing and modification. Rules should be added to deny hosts outside the control network from initiating connections with hosts on the control network. Rules should only allow devices internal to the control network the ability to establish connections outside the control network.

On the other hand, if the DMZ architecture is being used, then it is possible to configure the system so that no traffic will go directly between the corporate network and the control network. With a few special exceptions (noted below), all traffic from either side can terminate at the servers in the DMZ. This allows more flexibility in the protocols allowed through the firewall. For example, MODBUS/TCP might be used to communicate from the PLCs to the data historian, while HTTP might be used for communication between the historian and enterprise clients. Both protocols are inherently insecure, yet in this case they can be used safely because neither actually crosses between the two networks. An extension to this concept is the idea of using "disjoint" protocols in all control network to corporate network communications. That is, if a protocol is allowed between the control network and DMZ, then it is explicitly **not** allowed between the DMZ and corporate network. This design greatly reduces the chance of a worm such as Slammer actually making its way into the control network, because the worm would have to use two different exploits over two different protocols.

One area of considerable variation in practice is the control of outbound traffic from the control network, which could represent a significant risk if unmanaged. One example is Trojan horse software that uses HTTP tunneling to exploit poorly defined outbound rules. Thus, it is important that outbound rules be as stringent as inbound rules.

A summary of these follows:

Inbound traffic to the control system should be blocked. Access to devices inside the control system should be through a DMZ.

Outbound traffic through the control network firewall should be limited to essential communications only.

All outbound traffic from the control network to the corporate network should be source and destination-restricted by service and port.

In addition to these rules, the firewall should be configured with outbound filtering to stop forged IP packets from leaving the control network or the DMZ. In practice this is achieved by checking the source IP addresses of outgoing packets against the firewall's respective network interface address. The intent is to prevent the control network from being the source of spoofed (i.e., forged) communications, which are often used in DoS attacks. Thus, the firewalls should be configured to forward IP packets only if those packets have a correct source IP address for the control network or DMZ networks. Finally, Internet access by devices on the control network should be strongly discouraged.

In summary, the following should be considered as recommended practice for general firewall rule sets:

The base rule set should be deny all, permit none.

Ports and services between the control network environment and the corporate network should be enabled and permissions granted on a specific case-by-case basis. There should be a documented business justification with risk analysis and a responsible person for each permitted incoming or outgoing data flow.

All "permit" rules should be both IP address and TCP/UDP port specific, and stateful if appropriate.

All rules should restrict traffic to a specific IP address or range of addresses.

Traffic should be prevented from transiting directly from the control network to the corporate network. All traffic should terminate in the DMZ.

Any protocol allowed between the control network and DMZ should explicitly NOT be allowed between the DMZ and corporate networks (and vice-versa).

All outbound traffic from the control network to the corporate network should be source and destination-restricted by service and port.

Outbound packets from the control network or DMZ should be allowed only if those packets have a correct source IP address that is assigned to the control network or DMZ devices.

Control network devices should not be allowed to access the Internet.

Control networks should not be directly connected to the Internet, even if protected via a firewall.

All firewall management traffic should be carried on either a separate, secured management network (e.g., out of band) or over an encrypted network with multi-factor authentication. Traffic should also be restricted by IP address to specific management stations.

These should only be considered as guidelines. A careful assessment of each control environment is required before implementing any firewall rule sets.

5.6 Recommended Firewall Rules for Specific Services

Beside the general rules described above, it is difficult to outline all-purpose rules for specific protocols. The needs and recommended practices vary significantly between industries for any given protocol and should be analyzed on an organization-by-organization basis. The Industrial Automation Open Networking Association (IAONA) offers a template for conducting such an analysis [36], assessing each of the protocols commonly found in industrial environments in terms of function, security risk, worst case impact, and suggested measures. Below are summarized some of the key points from the IAONA document. The reader is advised to consult this document directly when developing rule sets.

5.6.1   Domain Name System (DNS)

Domain Name System (DNS) is primarily used to translate between domain names and IP addresses. For example, a DNS could map a domain name such as *control.com* to an IP address such as *192.168.1.1*. Most Internet services rely heavily on DNS, but its use on the control network is relatively rare at this time. In most cases there is little reason to allow DNS requests out of the control network to the corporate network and no reason to allow DNS requests into the control network. DNS requests from the control network to DMZ should be addressed on a case-by-case basis. Local DNS or the use of host files is recommended.

5.6.2   Hypertext Transfer Protocol (HTTP)

HTTP is the protocol underlying Web browsing services on the Internet. Like DNS, it is critical to most Internet services. It is seeing increasing use on the plant floor as well as an all-purpose query tool. Unfortunately, it has little inherent security, and many HTTP applications have vulnerabilities that can be exploited. HTTP can be a transport mechanism for many manually performed attacks and automated worms.

In general, HTTP should not be allowed to cross from the corporate to the control network. If it is, then HTTP proxies should be configured on the firewall to block all inbound scripts and Java applications. Incoming HTTP connections should not be allowed into the control network, as they pose significant security risks. If HTTP services into the control network are absolutely required, it is recommended that the more secure HTTPS be used instead and only to specific devices.

5.6.3   FTP and Trivial File Transfer Protocol (TFTP)

FTP and Trivial File Transfer Protocol (TFTP) are used for transferring files between devices. They are implemented on almost every platform including many SCADA systems, DCS, PLCs, and RTUs, because they are very well known and use minimum processing power. Unfortunately, neither protocol was created with security in mind; for FTP, the login password is not encrypted, and for TFTP, no login is required at all. Furthermore, some FTP implementations have a history of buffer overflow vulnerabilities. As a result, all TFTP communications should be blocked, while FTP communications should be allowed for outbound sessions only or if secured with additional token-based multi-factor authentication and an encrypted tunnel. More secure protocols, such as Secure FTP (SFTP) or Secure Copy (SCP), should be employed whenever possible.

5.6.4   Telnet

The telnet protocol defines an interactive, text-based communications session between a client and a host. It is mainly used for remote login and simple control services to systems with limited resources or to systems with limited needs for security. It is a severe security risk because all telnet traffic, including passwords, is unencrypted, and it can allow a remote individual considerable control over a device. Inbound telnet sessions from the corporate to the control network should be prohibited unless secured with token-based multi-factor authentication and an encrypted tunnel. Outbound telnet sessions should be allowed only over encrypted tunnels (e.g., VPN) to specific devices.

5.6.5   Simple Mail Transfer Protocol (SMTP)

SMTP is the primary e-mail transfer protocol on the Internet. E-mail messages often contain malware, so inbound e-mail should not be allowed to any control network device. Outbound SMTP mail messages from the control network to the corporate network are acceptable to send alert messages.

5.6.6 Simple Network Management Protocol (SNMP)

SNMP is used to provide network management services between a central management console and network devices such as routers, printers, and PLCs. Although SNMP is an extremely useful service for maintaining a network, it is very weak in security. Versions 1 and 2 of SNMP use unencrypted passwords to both read and configure devices (including devices such as PLCs), and in many cases the passwords are well known and cannot be changed. Version 3 is considerably more secure but is still limited in use. SNMP V1 & V2 commands both to and from the control network should be prohibited unless it is over a separate, secured management network whereas SNMP V3 commands may be able to be sent to the ICS using the security features inherent to V3.

5.6.7 Distributed Component Object Model (DCOM)

DCOM is the underlying protocol for both OLE for Process Control (OPC) and ProfiNet. It utilizes Microsoft's Remote Procedure Call (RPC) service which, when not patched, has many vulnerabilities. These vulnerabilities were the basis for the Blaster worm exploits. In addition, OPC, which utilizes DCOM, dynamically opens a wide range of ports (1024 to 65535) that can be extremely difficult to filter at the firewall. This protocol should only be allowed between control network and DMZ networks and explicitly blocked between the DMZ and corporate network. Also, users are advised to restrict the port ranges used by making registry modifications on devices using DCOM.

5.6.8 SCADA and Industrial Protocols

SCADA and industrial protocols, such as MODBUS/TCP, EtherNet/IP, and DNP3[18], are critical for communications to most control devices. Unfortunately, these protocols were designed without security built in and do not typically require any authentication to remotely execute commands on a control device. These protocols should only be allowed within the control network and not allowed to cross into the corporate network.

5.7 Network Address Translation (NAT)

Network address translation (NAT) is a service where IP addresses used on one side of a network device can be mapped to a different set on the other side on an as-needed basis. It was originally designed for IP address reduction purposes so that an organization with a large number of devices that occasionally needed Internet access could get by with a smaller set of assigned Internet addresses.

To do this, most NAT implementations rely on the premise that not every internal device is actively communicating with external hosts at a given moment. The firewall is configured to have a limited number of outwardly visible IP addresses. When an internal host seeks to communicate to an external host, the firewall remaps the internal IP address and port to one of the currently unused, more limited, public IP addresses, effectively concentrating outgoing traffic into fewer IP addresses. The firewall must track the state of each connection and how each private internal IP address and source port was remapped onto an outwardly visible IP address/port pair. When returning traffic reaches the firewall, the mapping is reversed and the packets forwarded to the proper internal host.

For example, a control network device may need to establish a connection with an external, non-control network host (for instance, to send a critical alert e-mail). NAT allows the internal IP address of the initiating control network host to be replaced by the firewall; subsequent return traffic packets are

---

[18] The DNP User Group is currently performing work in conjunction with IEC 62351 to extend the DNP3 protocol to provide strong authentication.

GUIDE TO INDUSTRIAL CONTROL SYSTEMS (ICS) SECURITY

remapped back to the internal IP address and sent to the appropriate control network device. More specifically, if the control network is assigned the private subnet 192.168.1.xxx and the Internet network expects the device to use the corporate assigned addresses in the range 192.6.yyy.zzz, then a NAT firewall will substitute (and track) a 192.6.yyy.zzz source address into every outbound IP packet generated by a control network device.

Producer-consumer protocols, such as EtherNet/IP and Foundation Fieldbus, are particularly troublesome because NAT does not support the multicast-based traffic that these protocols need to offer their full services.

In general, while NAT offers some distinct advantages, its impact on the actual industrial protocols and configuration should be assessed carefully before it is deployed. Furthermore, certain protocols are specifically broken by NAT because of the lack of direct addressing. For example, OPC requires special third-party tunneling software to work with NAT.

5.8   Specific ICS Firewall Issues

In addition to the issues with firewalls and ICS already discussed, there are some additional problems that need to be examined in more detail. The rest of this section discusses three specific areas of concern: the placement of data historians, remote access for ICS support, and multicast traffic.

5.8.1   Data Historians

The existence of shared control network/corporate network servers such as data historians and asset management servers can have a significant impact on firewall design and configuration. In three-zone systems the placement of these servers in a DMZ is relatively straightforward, but in two-zone designs the issues become complex. Placing the historian on the corporate side of the firewall means that a number of insecure protocols, such as MODBUS/TCP or DCOM, must be allowed through the firewall and that every control device reporting to the historian is exposed to the corporate side of the network. On the other hand, putting the historian on the control network side means other equally questionable protocols, such as HTTP or SQL, must be allowed through the firewall, and there is now a server accessible to nearly everyone in the organization sitting on the control network.

In general, the best solution is to avoid two-zone systems (no DMZ) and use a three-zone design, placing the data collector in the control network and the historian component in the DMZ; however, even this can prove problematic in some situations. Heavy access from the large numbers of users on the corporate network to a historian in the DMZ may tax the firewall's throughput capabilities. One potential solution is to install two servers: one on the control network to collect data from the control devices, and a second on the corporate network mirroring the first server and supporting client queries. The issue of how to time synchronize both historians will have to be addressed. This also requires a special hole to be put through the firewall to allow direct server-to-server communications, but if done correctly, this poses only minor risk.

5.8.2   Remote Support Access

Another issue for ICS firewall design is user and/or vendor remote access into the control network. Any users accessing the control network from remote networks should be required to authenticate using an appropriately strong mechanism such as token-based authentication. While it is possible for the controls group to set up their own remote access system with multi-factor authentication on the DMZ, in most organizations it is typically more efficient to use existing systems set up by the IT department. In this case a connection through the firewall from the IT remote access server is needed.

Remote support personnel connecting over the Internet or via dialup modems should use an encrypted protocol, such as running a corporate VPN connection client, application server, or secure HTTP access, and authenticate using a strong mechanism, such as a token based multi-factor authentication scheme, in order to connect to the general corporate network. Once connected, they should be required to authenticate a second time at the control network firewall using a strong mechanism, such as a token based multi-factor authentication scheme, to gain access to the control network. For organizations that do not allow any control traffic to traverse the corporate network in the clear, this could require a cascading, or secondary tunneling solutions, to gain access to the control network, such as a Secure Sockets Layer (SSL) or Transport Layer Security (TLS) VPN inside an IPsec VPN.

5.8.3   Multicast Traffic

Most industrial producer-consumer (or publisher-subscriber) protocols operating over Ethernet, such as EtherNet/IP and Foundation Fieldbus HSE, are IP multicast-based. The first advantage of IP multicasting is network efficiency; by not repeating the data transmission to the multiple destinations, a significant reduction in network load can occur. The second advantage is that the sending host need not be concerned with knowing every IP address of every destination host listening for the broadcast information. The third, and perhaps most important for industrial control purposes, is that a single multicast message offers far better capabilities for time synchronization between multiple control devices than multiple unicast messages.

If the source and destinations of a multicast packet are connected with no intervening routers or firewalls between them, the multicast transmission is relatively seamless. However, if the source and destinations are not on the same LAN, forwarding the multicast messages to a destination becomes more complicated. To solve the problem of multicast message routing, hosts need to join (or leave) a group by informing the multicast router on their network of the relevant group ID through the use of the Internet Group Management Protocol (IGMP). Multicast routers subsequently know of the members of multicast groups on their network and can decide whether or not to forward a received multicast message onto their network. A multicast routing protocol is also required. From a firewall administration perspective, monitoring and filtering IGMP traffic becomes another series of rule sets to manage, adding to the complexity of the firewall.

Another firewall issue related to multicasting is the use of NAT. A firewall performing NAT that receives a multicast packet from an external host has no reverse mapping for which internal group ID should receive the data. If IGMP-aware, it could broadcast it to every group ID it knows about, because one of them will be correct, but this could cause serious issues if an unintended control packet were broadcast to a critical node. The safest action for the firewall to take is to drop the packet. Thus, multicasting is generally considered NAT-unfriendly.

5.9   Single Points of Failure

Single points of failure can exist at any level of the ANSI/ISO stack. An example is PLC control of safety interlocks. Because security is usually being added to the ICS environment, an evaluation should be done to identity potential failure points and a risk assessment done to evaluate each point's exposure. Remediation methods can then be postulated and evaluated and a "risk versus reward" determination made and design and implementation done.

5.10 Redundancy and Fault Tolerance

ICS components or networks that are classified as critical to the organization have high availability requirements. One method of achieving high availability is through the use of redundancy. Additionally, if a component fails, it should fail in a manner that does not generate unnecessary traffic on the ICS, or does not cause another problem elsewhere, such as a cascading event.

The control system should have the ability to execute an appropriate fail-safe process upon the loss of communications with the ICS or the loss of the ICS itself. The organization should define what "loss of communications" means (e.g., 5 seconds, 5 minutes, etc. without communications). The organization should then, based on potential consequences, define the appropriate fail-safe process for their industry.

Backups should be performed using the "backup-in-depth" approach, with layers of backups (e.g., local, facility, disaster) that are time-sequenced such that rapid recent local backups are available for immediate use and secure backups are available to recover from a massive security incident. A mixture of backup/restore approaches and storage methods should be used to ensure that backups are rigorously produced, securely stored, and appropriately accessible for restoration.

5.11 Preventing Man-in-the-Middle Attacks

A man-in-the-middle attack requires knowledge of the protocol being manipulated. The Address Resolution Protocol (ARP) man-in-the-middle attack is a popular method for an adversary to gain access to the network flow of information on a target system. This is performed by attacking the network ARP cache tables of the controller and the workstation machines. Using the compromised computer on the control network, the adversary poisons the ARP tables on each host and informs them that they must route all their traffic through a specific IP and hardware address (i.e., the adversary's machine). By manipulating the ARP tables, the adversary can insert his machine between the two target machines and/or devices.

The ARP man-in-the-middle attack works by initiating gratuitous ARP commands to confuse each host (i.e., ARP poisoning). These ARP commands cause each of the two target hosts to use the MAC address of the adversary as the address for the other target host. When a successful man-in-the-middle attack is performed, the hosts on each side of the attack are unaware that their network data is taking a different route through the adversary's computer.

Once an adversary has successfully inserted their machine into the information stream, they now have full control over the data communications and could carry out several types of attacks. One possible attack method is the replay attack. In its simplest form, captured data from the control/HMI is modified to instantiate activity when received by the device controller. Captured data reflecting normal operations in the ICS could be played back to the operator as required. This would cause the operator's HMI to appear to be normal and the attack will go unobserved. During this replay attack the adversary could continue to send commands to the controller and/or field devices to cause an undesirable event while the operator is unaware of the true state of the system.

Another attack that could be carried out with the man-in-the-middle attack is sending false messages to the operator, and could take the form of a false negative or a false positive. This may cause the operator to take an action, such as flipping a breaker, when it is not required, or it may cause the operator to think everything is fine and not take an action when an action is required. The adversary could send commands to the operator's console indicating a system change, and when the operator follows normal procedures and attempts to correct the problem, the operator's action could cause an undesirable event. There are numerable variations of the modification and replay of control data which could impact the operations of the system.

Protocol manipulation and the man-in-the-middle attack are among the most popular ways to manipulate insecure protocols, such as those found in control systems. However, there are mitigation techniques [37] that can be applied to secure the systems through MAC address locking, static tables, encryption, and monitoring.

MAC Address Locking - The ARP man-in-the-middle attack requires the adversary to be connected to the local network or have control of a local computer on the network. Port security, also called MAC address locking, is one method to secure the physical connection at the end of each port on a network switch. High-end corporate class network switches usually have some kind of option for MAC address locking. MAC address locking is very effective against a rogue individual looking to physically plug into the internal network. Without port security, any open network jack on the wall could be used as an avenue onto the corporate network. Port security locks a specific MAC address to a specific port on a managed switch. If the MAC address does not match, the communication link is disabled and the intruder will not be able to achieve his goal. Some of the more advanced switches have an auto resetting option, which will reset the security measure if the original MAC is returned to the port.

Although port security is not attacker proof, it does add a layer of added security to the physical network. It also protects the local network from employees plugging un-patched and out-of-date systems onto the protected network. This reduces the number of target computers a remote adversary can access. These security measures not only protect against attacks from external networks but provide added physical protection as well.

Static Tables – An ICS network that stays relatively static could attempt to implement statically coded ARP tables. Most operating systems have the capability to statically code all of the MAC addresses into the ARP table on each computer. Statically coding the ARP tables on each computer prevents the adversary from changing them by sending ARP reply packets to the victim computer. While this technique is not feasible on a large and/or dynamic corporate network, the limited number of hosts on an ICS network could be effectively protected this way.

Encryption - As a longer term solution, systems should be designed to include encryption between devices in order to make it very difficult to reverse engineer protocols and forge packets on control system networks. Encrypting the communications between devices would make it nearly impossible to perform this attack. Protocols that provide strong authentication also provide resilience to man-in-the-middle attacks.

Monitoring - Monitoring for ARP poisoning provides an added layer of defense. There are several programs available (e.g., ARPwatch) that can monitor for changing MAC addresses through the ARP packets.

6. ICS Security Controls

Security controls are the management, operational, and technical controls (i.e., safeguards or countermeasures) prescribed for an informational system to protect the confidentiality, integrity, and availability of the system and its information. This section discusses the security controls specified in NIST SP 800-53, which was developed as part of the FISMA implementation project. See Appendix E for additional information regarding FISMA and the NIST-led implementation project.

NIST SP 800-53 provides guidelines for selecting and specifying security controls for information systems in support of Federal government information systems. Security controls are organized into three classes; management, operational, and technical controls. Each class is broken into several families of controls; each control contains a definition of the control, supplemental guidance, and possible enhancements that will increase the strength of a basic control.

NIST has initiated the Industrial Control System Security Project[19] in cooperation with the public and private sector ICS community to develop specific guidance on the application of NIST documents, including the security controls in NIST SP 800-53 to ICS. To facilitate the understanding of this approach, an effort is underway to develop a series of ICS cyber security case histories using actual ICS cyber security incidents. These case histories examine the NIST SP 800-53 ICS controls that were violated or not implemented, and postulate the potential mitigations that may have occurred if the controls had been implemented. ICS specific recommendations and guidance, if available, is provided in an outlined box for each set of controls in this section.

A single security product or technology cannot adequately protect an ICS. Securing an ICS is based on a combination of effective security policies and a properly configured set of security controls. An effective cyber security strategy for an ICS should apply defense-in-depth, a technique of layering security mechanisms so that the impact of a failure in any one mechanism is minimized. Use of such a strategy is explored within the security control discussions and their applications to ICS that follow.

6.1 Management Controls

Management controls are the security countermeasures for an ICS that focus on the management of risk and the management of information security. NIST SP 800-53 defines five families of controls within the Management controls class:

Security Assessment and Authorization (CA): assurance that the specified controls are implemented correctly, operating as intended, and producing the desired outcome.

Planning (PL): development and maintenance of a plan to address information system security by performing assessments, specifying and implementing security controls, assigning security levels, and responding to incidents

Risk Assessment (RA): the process of identifying risks to operations, assets, or individuals by determining the probability of occurrence, the resulting impact, and additional security controls that would mitigate this impact

System and Services Acquisition (SA): allocation of resources for information system security to be maintained throughout the systems life cycle and the development of acquisition policies based on risk assessment results including requirements, design criteria, test procedures, and associated documentation

---

[19] The Industrial Control System Security Project Web site is located at: http://csrc.nist.gov/groups/SMA/fisma/ics/

Program Management (PM): provides security controls at the organizational rather than the information-system level.

These management controls are discussed in more detail in the sections to follow. ICS specific recommendations and guidance, if available, is provided in an outlined box for each section.

6.1.1 Security Assessment and Authorization

The security controls that fall within the NIST SP 800-53 Assessment and Authorization (CA) family provide the basis for performing periodic assessments and providing certification of the security controls implemented in the information system to determine if the controls are implemented correctly, operating as intended, and producing the desired outcome to meet the system security requirements. A senior organizational official is responsible for accepting residual risk and authorizing system operation. These steps constitute accreditation. In addition, all security controls should be monitored on an ongoing basis. Monitoring activities include configuration management and control of information system components, security impact analysis of changes to the system, ongoing assessment of security controls, and status reporting.

Supplemental guidance for the CA controls can be found in the following documents:

NIST SP 800-12 provides guidance on security policies and procedures [38].

NIST SP 800-26 and 800-53A provide guidance on security control assessments [18][22].

NIST SP 800-37 provides guidance defining the information system boundary and security certification and accreditation of the information system [20].

6.1.2 Planning

A security plan is a formal document that provides an overview of the security requirements for an information system and describes the security controls in place or planned for meeting those requirements. The security controls that fall within the NIST SP 800-53 Planning (PL) family provide the basis for developing a security plan. These controls also address maintenance issues for periodically updating a security plan. A set of rules describes user responsibilities and expected behavior regarding information system usage with provision for signed acknowledgement from users indicating that they have read, understand, and agree to abide by the rules of behavior before authorizing access to the information system.

Supplemental guidance for the PL controls can be found in the following documents:

NIST SP 800-12 provides guidance on security policies and procedures [38].

NIST SP 800-18 provides guidance on preparing rules of behavior [17].

ICS Specific Recommendations and Guidance

A security plan for an ICS should build on appropriate existing IT security experience, programs, and practices. However, the critical differences between IT and ICS addressed in Section 3.1 will influence how security will be applied to the ICS. A forward-looking plan is needed to provide a method for

---

continuous security improvements. Whenever a new system is being designed and installed, it is imperative to take the time to address security throughout the lifecycle, from architecture to procurement to installation to maintenance to decommissioning. ICS security is a rapidly evolving field requiring the security planning process to constantly explore emerging ICS security capabilities as well as new threats that are identified by organizations such as the US-CERT Control Systems Security Center (CSSC).

6.1.3 Risk Assessment

Risk is a function of the likelihood of a given threat source exploiting a potential vulnerability and the resulting impact of a successful exploitation of the vulnerability. Risk assessment is the process of identifying risks to an organization's operations, assets, and individuals by determining the probability that an identified vulnerability will be exploited and the resulting impact. An assessment includes an evaluation of security controls that can mitigate each threat and the costs associated with implementing them. A risk assessment must also compare the cost of security with the costs associated with an incident.

Achieving an acceptable level of risk is a process of reducing the probability of an incident that is accomplished by mitigating or eliminating vulnerabilities that can be exploited as well as consequences resulting from an incident. Prioritization of vulnerabilities must be based on cost and benefit with an objective to provide a business case for implementing at least a minimum set of control system security requirements to reduce risk to an acceptable level. A mistake often made during a risk assessment is to select technically interesting vulnerabilities without taking into account the level of risk associated with them. Vulnerabilities should be assessed and rated for risk before trying to select and implement security controls on them.

The security controls that fall within the NIST SP 800-53 Risk Assessment (RA) family provide policy and procedures to develop, distribute, and maintain a documented risk assessment policy that describes purpose, scope, roles, responsibilities, and compliance as well as policy implementation procedures. An information system and associated data is categorized based on the security objectives and a range of risk levels. A risk assessment is performed to identify risks and the magnitude of harm that could result from the unauthorized access, use, disclosure, disruption, modification, or destruction of an information system and data. Also included in these controls are mechanisms for keeping risk assessments up-to-date and performing periodic testing and vulnerability assessments.

In the FISMA Risk Framework shown in Figure E-1 in Appendix E, the risk assessment process is applied after the Security Categorization activity and baseline Security Control Selection activity. Risk assessment is performed in the Security Control Refinement activity to determine if the selected security controls need to be enhanced or expanded beyond the baseline security controls. NIST SP 800-30, *Risk Management Guide for Information Technology Systems* (currently under revision) provides a risk assessment methodology, which includes the following steps:

1. System characterization – produces a picture of the information system environment, and delineation of system boundaries

2. Threat identification – produces a threat statement containing a list of threat-sources that could exploit system vulnerabilities

3. Vulnerability identification – produces a list of the system vulnerabilities that could be exercised by the potential threat sources

4. Control analysis – produces a list of the planned controls used for the information system to mitigate the likelihood of a vulnerability being exercised and reduce the impact of such an adverse event.

5. Likelihood determination – produces a likelihood rating (High, Medium, or Low) that indicates the probability that a potential vulnerability may be exercised

6. Impact analysis – produces a magnitude of impact (High, Medium, or Low) resulting from the exploitation of a vulnerability.

7. Risk determination – produces measurement for risk based on a scale of High, Medium, or Low

8. Control recommendations – produces recommendations of security controls and alternative solutions to mitigate risk

9. Results documentation – produces a risk assessment report that describes the threats and vulnerabilities, measurement of risk, and provides recommendations for control implementation.

Supplemental guidance for the RA controls can be found in the following documents:

NIST SP 800-12 provides guidance on security policies and procedures [38].

NIST SP 800-39 provides guidance on conducting risk assessments and updates [19].

NIST SP 800-40 provides guidance on handling security patches [39].

NIST SP 800-115 provides guidance on network security testing [40].

NIST SP 800-60 provides guidance on determining security categories for information types [24].

ICS Specific Recommendations and Guidance

Organizations must consider the potential consequences resulting from an incident on an ICS. Well-defined policies and procedures lead to mitigation techniques designed to thwart incidents and manage the risk to eliminate or minimize the consequences. The potential degradation of the physical plant, economic status, or stakeholder/national confidence could justify mitigation. For an ICS, a very important aspect of the risk assessment is to determine the value of the data that is flowing from the control network to the corporate network. In instances where pricing decisions are determined from this data, the data could have a very high value. The fiscal justification for mitigation has to be derived by comparing the mitigation cost to the effects of the consequence. However, it is not possible to define a one-size-fits-all set of security requirements. A very high level of security may be achievable but undesirable in many situations because of the loss of functionality and other associated costs. A well-thought-out security implementation is a balance of risk versus cost. In some situations the risk may be safety, health, or environment-related rather than purely economic. The risk may result in an unrecoverable consequence rather than a temporary financial setback

---

6.1.4 System and Services Acquisition

The security controls that fall within the NIST SP 800-53 System and Services Acquisition (SA) family provide the basis for developing policies and procedures for acquisition of resources required to adequately protect an information system. These acquisitions are based on security requirements and security specifications. As part of the acquisition procedures, an information system is managed using a system development life cycle methodology that includes information security considerations. As part of acquisition, adequate documentation must be maintained on the information system and constituent components.

The SA family also addresses outsourced systems and the inclusion of adequate security controls by vendors as specified by the supported organization. Vendors are also responsible for configuration management and security testing for these outsourced information systems.

Supplemental guidance for the SA controls can be found in the following documents:

NIST SP 800-12 provides guidance on security policies and procedures [38].

NIST SP 800-23 provides guidance on the acquisition and use of tested/evaluated information technology products [41].

NIST SP 800-27 provides guidance on engineering principles for information system security [42].

NIST SP 800-35 provides guidance on information technology security services [43].

NIST SP 800-36 provides guidance on the selection of information security products [44].

NIST SP 800-64 provides guidance on security considerations in the system development life cycle [45].

NIST SP 800-65 provides guidance on integrating security into the capital planning and investment control process [46].

NIST SP 800-70 provides guidance on configuration settings for information technology products [25].

ICS Specific Recommendations and Guidance

The security requirements of an organization outsourcing the management and control of all or some of its information systems, networks, and desktop environments should be addressed in a contract agreed between the parties. External suppliers that have an impact on the security of the organization must be held to the same security policies and procedures to maintain the overall level of ICS security. Security policies and procedures of second and third-tier suppliers should also be in compliance with corporate cyber security policies and procedures in the case that they impact ICS security.

The SCADA and Control System Procurement Project [47] has developed a procurement language for specifying security requirements when procuring new systems or maintaining existing systems.

6.1.5 Program Management

The security controls that fall within the NIST SP 800-53 Program Management (PM) focus on the organization-wide information security requirements that are independent of any particular information system and are essential for managing information security programs.

6.2 Operational Controls

Operational controls are the security countermeasures for an ICS that are primarily implemented and executed by people as opposed to systems. NIST SP 800-53 defines nine families of controls within the Operational controls class:

Personnel Security (PS): policies and procedures for personnel position categorization, screening, transfer, penalty, and termination; also addresses third-party personnel security.

Physical and Environmental Protection (PE): policies and procedures addressing physical, transmission, and display access control as well as environmental controls for conditioning (e.g., temperature, humidity) and emergency provisions (e.g., shutdown, power, lighting, fire protection).

Contingency Planning (CP): policies and procedures designed to maintain or restore business operations, including computer operations, possibly at an alternate location, in the event of emergencies, system failures, or disaster.

Configuration Management (CM): policies and procedures for controlling modifications to hardware, firmware, software, and documentation to ensure the information system is protected against improper modifications prior to, during, and after system implementation.

Maintenance (MA): policies and procedures to manage all maintenance aspects of an information system.

System and Information Integrity (SI): policies and procedures to protect information systems and their data from design flaws and data modification using functionality verification, data integrity checking, intrusion detection, malicious code detection, and security alert and advisory controls.

Media Protection (MP): policies and procedures to ensure secure handling of media. Controls cover access, labeling, storage, transport, sanitization, destruction, and disposal.

Incident Response (IR): policies and procedures pertaining to incident response training, testing, handling, monitoring, reporting, and support services.

Awareness and Training (AT): policies and procedures to ensure that all information system users are given appropriate security training relative to their usage of the system and that accurate training records are maintained.

These operational controls are discussed in more detail in the sections to follow. ICS specific recommendations and guidance, if available, is provided in an outlined box for each section.

6.2.1 Personnel Security

The security controls that fall within the NIST SP 800-53 Personnel Security (PS) family provide policies and procedures to reduce the risk of human error, theft, fraud, or other intentional or unintentional misuse of information systems.

Supplemental guidance for the PS controls can be found in the following documents:

NIST SP 800-12 provides guidance on security policies and procedures [38].

NIST SP 800-35 provides guidance on information technology security services [43].

NIST SP 800-73 provides guidance on interfaces for personal identity verification [48].

NIST SP 800-76 provides guidance on biometrics for personal identity verification [49].

Personnel security measures are meant to reduce the possibility and risk of human error, theft, fraud, or other intentional or unintentional misuse of informational assets. There are three main aspects to personnel security:

Hiring Policies. This includes pre-employment screening such as background checks, the interview process, employment terms and conditions, complete job descriptions and detailing of duties, terms and condition of employment, and legal rights and responsibilities of employees or contractors.

Organization Policies and Practices. These include security policies, information classification, document and media maintenance and handling policies, user training, acceptable usage policies for organization assets, periodic employee performance reviews, appropriate background checks, and any other policies and actions that detail expected and required behavior of organization employees, contractors, and visitors. Organization policies to be enforced should be written down and readily available to all workers through an employee handbook, distributed as e-mail notices, located in a centralized resource area, or posted directly at a worker's area of responsibility.

Terms and Conditions of Employment. This category includes job and position responsibilities, notification to employees of terminable offenses, disciplinary actions and punishments, and periodic employee performance reviews.

ICS Specific Recommendations and Guidance

Positions should be categorized with a risk designation and screening criteria, and individuals filling a position should be screened against this criteria as well as complete an access agreement before being granted access to an information system. Personnel should be screened for the critical positions controlling and maintaining the ICS.

6.2.2 Physical and Environmental Protection

The security controls that fall within the NIST SP 800-53 Physical and Environmental Protection (PE) family provide policy and procedures for all physical access to an information system including designated entry/exit points, transmission media, and display media. These include controls for monitoring physical access, maintaining logs, and handling visitors. This family also includes controls for the deployment and management of emergency protection controls such as emergency shutdown of the IT system, backup for power and lighting, controls for temperature and humidity, and protection against fire and water damage.

Supplemental guidance for the PE controls can be found in the following documents:

NIST SP 800-12 provides guidance on security policies and procedures [38].

NIST SP 800-46 provides guidance on telecommuting and broadband communication security [50].

Physical security measures are designed to reduce the risk of accidental or deliberate loss or damage to plant assets and the surrounding environment. The assets being safeguarded may be physical assets such as tools and plant equipment, the environment, the surrounding community, and intellectual property, including proprietary data such as process settings and customer information. The deployment of physical security controls is often subject to environmental, safety, regulatory, legal, and other requirements that must be identified and addressed specific to a given environment. The subject of deploying physical security controls is vast and needs to be specific to the type of protection needed.

ICS Specific Recommendations and Guidance

The physical protection of the cyber components and data associated with the ICS must be addressed as part of the overall security of a plant. Security at many ICS facilities is closely tied to plant safety. A primary goal is to keep people out of hazardous situations without preventing them from doing their job or carrying out emergency procedures.

Gaining physical access to a control room or control system components often implies gaining logical access to the process control system as well. Likewise, having logical access to systems such as main servers and control room computers allows an adversary to exercise control over the physical process. If computers are readily accessible, and they have removable media drives (e.g., floppy disks, compact discs, external hard drives) or USB ports, the drives can be fitted with locks or removed from the computers and USB ports disabled. Depending on security needs and risks, it might also be prudent to disable or physically protect power buttons to prevent unauthorized use. For maximum security, servers should be placed in locked areas and authentication mechanisms (such as keys) protected. Also, the network devices on the ICS network, including switches, routers, network jacks, servers, workstations, and controllers, should be located in a secured area that can only be accessed by authorized personnel. The secured area should also be compatible with the environmental requirements of the devices.

A defense-in-depth solution to physical security should include the following attributes:

Protection of Physical Locations. Classic physical security considerations typically refer to a ringed architecture of layered security measures. Creating several physical barriers, both active and passive, around buildings, facilities, rooms, equipment, or other informational assets, establishes these physical security perimeters. Physical security controls meant to protect physical locations include fences, anti-vehicle ditches, earthen mounds, walls, reinforced barricades, gates, or other measures. Most organizations include this layered model by preventing access to the plant first by the use of fences, guard shacks, gates, and locked doors.

Access Control. Access control systems should ensure that only authorized people have access to controlled spaces. An access control system should be flexible. The need for access may be based on time (day vs. night shift), level of training, employment status, work assignment, plant status, and a myriad of other factors. A system must be able to verify that persons being granted access are who they say they are (usually using something the person has, such as an access card or key; something they know, such as a personal identification number (PIN); or something they are, using a biometric device). Access control should be highly reliable, yet not interfere with the routine or

---

emergency duties of plant personnel. Integration of access control into the process system allows a view into not only security access, but also physical and personnel asset tracking, dramatically accelerating response time in emergencies, helping to direct individuals to safe locations, and improving overall productivity. Within an area, access to network and computer cabinets should be limited to only those who have a need, such as network technicians and engineers, or computer maintenance staff. Equipment cabinets should be locked and wiring should be neat and within cabinets. Consider keeping all computers in secure racks and using peripheral extender technology to connect human-machine interfaces to the racked computers.

Access Monitoring Systems. Access monitoring systems include still and video cameras, sensors, and various types of identification systems. Examples of these systems include cameras that monitor parking lots, convenience stores, or airline security. These devices do not specifically prevent access to a particular location; rather, they store and record either the physical presence or the lack of physical presence of individuals, vehicles, animals, or other physical entities. Adequate lighting should be provided based on the type of access monitoring device deployed.

Access Limiting Systems. Access limiting systems may employ a combination of devices to physically control or prevent access to protected resources. Access limiting systems include both active and passive security devices such as fences, doors, safes, gates, and guards. They are often coupled with identification and monitoring systems to provide role-based access for specific individuals or groups of individuals.

People and Asset Tracking. Locating people and vehicles in a large installation is important for safety reasons, and it is increasingly important for security reasons as well. Asset location technologies can be used to track the movements of people and vehicles within the plant, to ensure that they stay in authorized areas, to identify personnel needing assistance, and to support emergency response.

Environmental Factors. In addressing the security needs of the system and data, it is important to consider environmental factors. For example, if a site is dusty, systems should be placed in a filtered environment. This is particularly important if the dust is likely to be conductive or magnetic, as in the case of sites that process coal or iron. If vibration is likely to be a problem, systems should be mounted on rubber bushings to prevent disk crashes and wiring connection problems. In addition, the environments containing systems and media (e.g., backup tapes, floppy disks) should have stable temperature and humidity. An alarm to the process control system should be generated when environmental specifications such as temperature and humidity are exceeded.

Environmental Control Systems. Heating, ventilation, and air conditioning (HVAC) systems for control rooms must support plant personnel during normal operation and emergency situations, which could include the release of toxic substances. Fire systems must be carefully designed to avoid causing more harm than good (e.g., to avoid mixing water with incompatible products). HVAC and fire systems have significantly increased roles in security that arise from the interdependence of process control and security. For example, fire prevention and HVAC systems that support industrial control computers need to be protected against cyber incidents.

Power. Reliable power for the ICS is essential, so an uninterruptible power supply (UPS) should be provided. If the site has an emergency generator, the UPS battery life may only need to be a few seconds; however, if the site relies on external power, the UPS battery life may need to be hours. It should be sized, at a minimum, so that the system can be shutdown safely.

6.2.2.1 Control Center/Control Room

ICS Specific Recommendations and Guidance

Providing physical security for the control center/control room is essential to reduce the potential of many threats. Control centers/control rooms frequently have consoles continuously logged onto the primary control server, where speed of response and continual view of the plant is of utmost importance. These areas will often contain the servers themselves, other critical computer nodes, and sometimes plant controllers. It is essential that access to these areas be limited to authorized users only, using authentication methods such as smart or magnetic identity cards or biometric devices. In extreme cases, it may be considered necessary to make the control center/control room blast-proof, or to provide an offsite emergency control center/control room so that control can be maintained if the primary control center/control room becomes uninhabitable.

6.2.2.2 Portable Devices

ICS Specific Recommendations and Guidance

Computers and computerized devices used for ICS functions (such as PLC programming) should never be allowed to leave the ICS area. Laptops, portable engineering workstations and handhelds (e.g., 375 HART communicator) should be tightly secured and should never be allowed to be used outside the ICS network. Antivirus and patch management should be kept current.

6.2.2.3 Cabling

ICS Specific Recommendations and Guidance

Cabling design and implementation for the control network should be addressed in the cyber security plan. Unshielded twisted pair communications cable, while acceptable for the office environment, is generally not suitable for the plant environment due to its susceptibility to interference from magnetic fields, radio waves, temperature extremes, moisture, dust, and vibration. Industrial RJ-45 connectors should be used in place of other types of twisted pair connectors to provide protection against moisture, dust and vibration. Fiber-optic cable and coaxial cable are often better network cabling choices for the control network because they are immune to many of the typical environmental conditions including electrical and radio frequency interference found in an industrial control environment. Cable and connectors should be color-coded and labeled so that the ICS and IT networks are clearly delineated and the potential for an inadvertent cross-connect is reduced. Cable runs should be installed so that access is minimized (i.e., limited to authorized personnel only) and equipment should be installed in locked cabinets with adequate ventilation and air filtration.

6.2.3 Contingency Planning

Contingency plans are designed to maintain or restore business operations, including computer operations, possibly at an alternate location, in the event of emergencies, system failures, or disaster. The security controls that fall within the NIST SP 800-53 Contingency Planning (CP) family provide policies and procedures to implement a contingency plan by specifying roles and responsibilities, assigning personnel and activities associated with restoring the information system after a disruption or failure. Along with planning, controls also exist for contingency training, testing, and plan update, and for backup information processing and storage sites.

Supplemental guidance for the CP controls can be found in the following documents:

NIST SP 800-12 provides guidance on security policies and procedures [38].

NIST SP 800-34 provides guidance on contingency planning [51].

ICS Specific Recommendations and Guidance

Contingency plans should cover the full range of failures or problems that could be caused by cyber incidents. Contingency plans should include procedures for restoring systems from known valid backups, separating systems from all non-essential interferences and connections that could permit cyber security intrusions, and alternatives to achieve necessary interfaces and coordination. Employees should be trained and familiar with the contents of the contingency plans. Contingency plans should be periodically reviewed with employees responsible for restoration of the ICS, and tested to ensure that they continue to meet their objectives. Organizations also have business continuity plans and disaster recovery plans that are closely related to contingency plans. Because business continuity and disaster recovery plans are particularly important for ICS, they are described in more detail in the sections to follow.

6.2.3.1 Business Continuity Planning

Business continuity planning addresses the overall issue of maintaining or reestablishing production in the case of an interruption. These interruptions may take the form of a natural disaster (e.g., hurricane, tornado, earthquake, flood), an unintentional man-made event (e.g., accidental equipment damage, fire or explosion, operator error), an intentional man-made event (e.g., attack by bomb, firearm or vandalism, attacker or virus), or an equipment failure. From a potential outage perspective, this may involve typical time spans of days, weeks, or months to recover from a natural disaster, or minutes or hours to recover from a malware infection or a mechanical/electrical failure. Because there is often a separate discipline that deals with reliability and electrical/mechanical maintenance, some organizations choose to define business continuity in a way that excludes these sources of failure. Because business continuity also deals primarily with the long-term implications of production outages, some organizations also choose to place a minimum interruption limit on the risks to be considered. For the purposes of ICS cyber security, it is recommended that neither of these constraints be made. Long-term outages (disaster recovery) and short-term outages (operational recovery) should both be considered. Because some of these potential interruptions involve man-made events, it is also important to work collaboratively with the physical security organization to understand the relative risks of these events and the physical security countermeasures that are in place to prevent them. It is also important for the physical security organization to understand which areas of a production site house data acquisition and control systems that might have higher-level risks.

Before creating a business continuity plan (BCP) to deal with potential outages, it is important to specify the recovery objectives for the various systems and subsystems involved based on typical business needs. There are two distinct types of objectives: system recovery and data recovery. System recovery involves the recovery of communication links and processing capabilities, and it is usually specified in terms of a Recovery Time Objective (RTO). This is defined as the time required to recover the required communication links and processing capabilities. Data recovery involves the recovery of data describing production or product conditions in the past and is usually specified in terms of a Recovery Point Objective (RPO). This is defined as the longest period of time for which an absence of data can be tolerated.

Once the recovery objectives are defined, a list of potential interruptions should be created and the recovery procedure developed and described. For most of the smaller scale interruptions, repair and replace activities based on a critical spares inventory will prove adequate to meet the recovery objectives. When this is not true, contingency plans need to be developed. Due to the potential cost and importance of these contingency plans, they should be reviewed with the managers responsible for business continuity planning to verify that they are justified. Once the recovery procedures are documented, a schedule should be developed to test part or all of the recovery procedures. Particular attention must be paid to the verification of backups of system configuration data and product or production data. Not only should these be tested when they are produced, but the procedures followed for their storage should also be reviewed periodically to verify that the backups are kept in environmental conditions that will not render them unusable and that they are kept in a secure location, so they can be quickly obtained by authorized individuals when needed.

6.2.3.2 Disaster Recovery Planning

ICS Specific Recommendations and Guidance

A disaster recovery plan (DRP) is essential to continued availability of the ICS. The DRP should include the following items:

Required response to events or conditions of varying duration and severity that would activate the recovery plan

Procedures for operating the ICS in manual mode with all external electronic connections severed until secure conditions can be restored

Roles and responsibilities of responders

Processes and procedures for the backup and secure storage of information

Complete and up-to-date logical network diagram

Personnel list for authorized physical and cyber access to the ICS

Communication procedure and list of personnel to contact in the case of an emergency including ICS vendors, network administrators, ICS support personnel, etc

Current configuration information for all components

The plan should also indicate requirements for the timely replacement of components in the case of an emergency. If possible, replacements for hard-to-obtain critical components should be kept in inventory.

The security plan should define a comprehensive backup and restore policy. In formulating this policy, the following should be considered:

The speed at which data or the system must be restored. This requirement may justify the need for a redundant system, spare offline computer, or valid file system backups.

The frequency at which critical data and configurations are changing. This will dictate the frequency and completeness of backups.

The safe onsite and offsite storage of full and incremental backups

The safe storage of installation media, license keys, and configuration information

Identification of individuals responsible for performing, testing, storing, and restoring backups

6.2.4 Configuration Management

Configuration management policy and procedures are used to control modifications to hardware, firmware, software, and documentation to ensure the information system is protected against improper modifications prior to, during, and after system implementation. The security controls that fall within the NIST SP 800-53 Configuration Management (CM) family provide policy and procedures for establishing baseline controls for information systems. Controls are also specified for maintaining, monitoring, and documenting configuration control changes. There should be restricted access to configuration settings, and security settings of IT products should be set to the most restrictive mode consistent with ICS operational requirements.

Supplemental guidance for the CM controls can be found in the following documents:

NIST SP 800-12 provides guidance on security policies and procedures [38].

NIST SP 800-70 provides guidance on configuration settings for IT products [25].

ICS Specific Recommendations and Guidance

A formal change management program should be established and procedures used to insure that all modifications to an ICS network meet the same security requirements as the original components identified in the asset evaluation and the associated risk assessment and mitigation plans. Risk assessment should be performed on all changes to the ICS network that could affect security, including configuration changes, the addition of network components, and installation of software. Changes to policies and procedures may also be required. The current ICS network configuration must always be known and documented.

6.2.5 Maintenance

The security controls that fall within the NIST SP 800-53 Maintenance (MA) family provide policy and procedure for performing routine and preventative maintenance on the components of an information system. This includes the usage of maintenance tools (both local and remote) and management of maintenance personnel.

Supplemental guidance for the MA controls can be found in the following documents:

NIST SP 800-12 provides guidance on security policies and procedures [38].

NIST SP 800-63 provides guidance on electronic authentication for remote maintenance [52].

6.2.6 System and Information Integrity

Maintaining system and information integrity assures that sensitive data has not been modified or deleted in an unauthorized and undetected manner. The security controls that fall within the NIST SP 800-53 System and Information Integrity (SI) family provide policies and procedures for identifying, reporting, and correcting information system flaws. Controls exist for malicious code detection, spam and spyware protection, and intrusion detection, although they may not be appropriate for all ICS applications. Also provided are controls for receiving security alerts and advisories, and the verification of security functions on the information system. In addition, there are controls within this family to detect and protect against unauthorized changes to software and data, provide restrictions to data input and output, and check for the accuracy, completeness, and validity of data as well as handle error conditions, although they may not be appropriate for all ICS applications.

Supplemental guidance for the SI controls can be found in the following documents:

NIST SP 800-12 provides guidance on security policies and procedures [38].

NIST SP 800-40 provides guidance on security patch installation [39].

NIST SP 800-94 provides guidance on Intrusion Detection and Prevention (IDP) Systems [54].

ICS Specific Recommendations and Guidance

Controls exist for malicious code detection, spam and spyware protection, and intrusion detection, although they may not be appropriate for all ICS applications. ICS specific recommendations and guidance for these controls are included in Sections 6.2.6.1 through 6.2.6.3.

6.2.6.1 Malicious Code Detection

Antivirus products evaluate files on a computer's storage devices against an inventory of known malware signature files. If one of the files on a computer matches the profile of a known virus, the virus is removed through a disinfection process (e.g., quarantine, deletion) so it cannot infect other local files or communicate across a network to infect other files. Antivirus software can be deployed on workstations, servers, firewalls and handheld devices.

ICS Specific Recommendations and Guidance

Antivirus tools only function effectively when installed, configured, running full-time, and maintained properly against the state of known attack methods and payloads. While antivirus tools are common security practice in IT computer systems, their use with ICS may require adopting special practices including compatibility checks, change management issues, and performance impact metrics. These special practices should be utilized whenever new signatures or new versions of antivirus software are installed.

Major ICS vendors recommend and even support the use of particular antivirus tools. In some cases, control system vendors may have performed regression testing across their product line for supported versions of a particular antivirus tool and also provide associated installation and configuration documentation. There is also an effort to develop a general set of guidelines and test procedures focused on ICS performance impacts to fill the gaps where ICS and antivirus vendor guidance is not available [55].

Generally:

Windows, Unix, Linux systems, etc. used as consoles, engineering workstations, data historians, HMIs and general purpose SCADA and backup servers can be secured just like commercial IT equipment: install push- or auto-updated antivirus and patch management software with updates distributed via an antivirus server and patch management server located inside the process control network and auto-updated from the IT network

Follow vendor recommendations on all other servers and computers (DCS, PLC, instruments) that have time-dependent code, modified or extended the operating system or any other change that makes it different from any standard PC that one could buy at an office supply or computer store. Expect the vendor to make periodic maintenance releases that include security patches.

6.2.6.2 Intrusion Detection and Prevention

Intrusion detection systems (IDS) monitor events on a network, such as traffic patterns, or a system, such as log entries or file accesses, so that they can identify an intruder breaking into or attempting to break into a system [56]. IDS ensure that unusual activity such as new open ports, unusual traffic patterns, or changes to critical operating system files is brought to the attention of the appropriate security personnel.

The two most commonly used types of IDS are:

Network-Based IDS. These systems monitor network traffic and generate alarms when they identify traffic that they deem to be an attack.

Host-Based IDS. This software monitors one or more types of characteristics of a system, such as application log file entries, system configuration changes, and access to sensitive data on a system and responds with an alarm or countermeasure when a user attempts to breach security.

ICS Specific Recommendations and Guidance

An effective IDS deployment typically involves both host-based and network-based IDS. In the current ICS environment, network-based IDS are most often deployed between the control network and the corporate network in conjunction with a firewall; host-based IDS are most often deployed on the computers that use general-purpose OSs or applications such as HMIs, SCADA servers, and engineering workstations. Properly configured, an IDS can greatly enhance the security management team's ability to detect attacks entering or leaving the system, thereby improving security. They can also potentially improve a control network's efficiency by detecting non-essential traffic on the network. However, even when IDS are implemented, security staff can primarily recognize individual attacks, as opposed to organized patterns of attacks over time. Additionally, care should be given to not confuse unusual ICS activity, such as during transient conditions, as an attack.

Current IDS and IPS products are effective in detecting and preventing well-known Internet attacks, but until recently they have not addressed ICS protocol attacks. IDS and IPS vendors are beginning to develop and incorporate attack signatures for various ICS protocols such as Modbus, DNP, and ICCP. [57] Appendix D provides some additional information on emerging IDS capabilities.

6.2.6.3 Patch Management

Patches are additional pieces of code that have been developed to address specific problems or flaws in existing software. Vulnerabilities are flaws that can be exploited, enabling unauthorized access to IT systems or enabling users to have access to greater privileges than authorized.

A systematic approach to managing and using software patches can help organizations to improve the overall security of their IT systems in a cost-effective way. Organizations that actively manage and use software patches can reduce the chances that the vulnerabilities in their IT systems can be exploited; in addition, they can save time and money that might be spent in responding to vulnerability-related incidents.

NIST SP 800-40 Version 2 provides guidance for organizational security managers who are responsible for designing and implementing security patch and vulnerability management programs and for testing the effectiveness of the programs in reducing vulnerabilities. The guidance is also useful to system administrators and operations personnel who are responsible for applying and testing patches and for deploying solutions to vulnerability problems.

ICS Specific Recommendations and Guidance

Applying patches to OS components creates another situation where significant care should be exercised in the ICS environment. Patches should be adequately tested (e.g., off-line on a comparable ICS) to determine the acceptability of side effects. Regression testing is advised. It is not uncommon for patches to have an adverse effect on other software. A patch may remove a vulnerability, but it can also introduce a greater risk from a production or safety perspective. Patching the vulnerability may also change the way the OS or application works with control applications, causing the control application to lose some of its functionality. Another issue is that many ICS utilize older versions of operating systems that are no longer supported by the vendor. Consequently, available patches may not be applicable. Organizations should implement a systematic, accountable, and documented ICS patch management process for managing exposure to vulnerabilities.

Once the decision is made to deploy a patch, there are other tools that automate this process from a centralized server and with confirmation that the patch has been deployed correctly. Consider separating the automated process for ICS patch management from the automated process for non-ICS applications. Patching should be scheduled to occur during planned ICS outages.

6.2.7 Media Protection

The security controls that fall within the NIST SP 800-53 Media Protection (MP) family provide policies and procedures for limiting the access to media to authorized users. Controls also exist for labeling media for distribution and handling requirements, as well as storage, transport, sanitization (removal of information from digital media), destruction, and disposal of the media.

Supplemental guidance for the MP controls can be found in the following documents:

NIST SP 800-12 provides guidance on security policies and procedures [38].

NIST SP 800-88 provides guidance on appropriate sanitization equipment, techniques, and procedures [77].

ICS Specific Recommendations and Guidance

Media assets include removable media and devices such as floppy disks, CDs, DVDs and USB memory sticks, as well as printed reports and documents. Physical security controls should address specific requirements for the safe and secure maintenance of these assets and provide specific guidance for transporting, handling, and erasing or destroying these assets. Security requirements could include safe storage from loss, fire, theft, unintentional distribution, or environmental damage. If an adversary gains access to backup media associated with an ICS, it could provide valuable data for launching an attack. Recovering an authentication file from the backups might allow an adversary to run password cracking tools and extract usable passwords. In addition, the backups typically contain machine names, IP addresses, software version numbers, usernames, and other data useful in planning an attack.

The use of any unauthorized CDs, DVDs, floppy disks, USB memory sticks, or similar removable media on any node that is part of or connected to the ICS should not be permitted in order to prevent the introduction of malware or the inadvertent loss or theft of data. Where the system components use unmodified industry standard protocols, mechanized policy management software can be used to enforce media protection policy.

6.2.8 Incident Response

An incident response plan is documentation of a predetermined set of instructions or procedures to detect, respond to, and limit consequences of incidents against an organization's information systems. Response should be measured first and foremost against the "service being provided", not just the system that was compromised. If an incident is discovered, there should be a quick risk assessment performed to evaluate the effect of both the attack and the options to respond. For example, one possible response option is to physically isolate the system under attack. However, this may have such a dire impact on the service that it is dismissed as not viable.

The security controls that fall within the NIST SP 800-53 Incident Response (IR) family provide policies and procedures for incident response monitoring, handling, and reporting. The handling of a security incident includes preparation, detection and analysis, containment, eradication, and recovery. Controls also cover incident response training for personnel and testing the incident response capability for an information system.

Supplemental guidance for the IR controls can be found in the following documents:

NIST SP 800-12 provides guidance on security policies and procedures [38].

NIST SP 800-61 provides guidance on incident handling and reporting [58].

NIST SP 800-83 provides guidance on malware incident prevention and handling [59].

ICS Specific Recommendations and Guidance

Regardless of the steps taken to protect an ICS, it is always possible that it may be compromised by an intentional or unintentional incident. The following symptoms can arise from normal network problems, but when several symptoms start to appear, a pattern may indicate the ICS is under attack and may be worth investigating further. If the adversary is skilled, it may not be very obvious that an attack is underway.

The symptoms of an incident could include any of the following:

Unusually heavy network traffic

Out of disk space or significantly reduced free disk space

Unusually high CPU usage

Creation of new user accounts

Attempted or actual use of administrator-level accounts

Locked-out accounts

Account in-use when the user is not at work

Cleared log files

Full log files with unusually large number of events

Antivirus or IDS alerts

Disabled antivirus software and other security controls

Unexpected patch changes

Machines connecting to outside IP addresses

Requests for information about the system (social engineering attempts)

Unexpected changes in configuration settings

Unexpected system shutdown.

To minimize the effects of these intrusions, it is necessary to plan a response. Incident response planning defines procedures to be followed when an intrusion occurs. NIST SP 800-61, *Computer Security Incident Handling Guide*, provides guidance on incident response planning, which might include the following items:

Classification of Incidents. The various types of ICS incidents should be identified and classified as to potential impact so that a proper response can be formulated for each potential incident.

Response Actions. There are several responses that can be taken in the event of an incident. These range from doing nothing to full system shutdown (although full shutdown of an ICS is a highly unlikely response). The response taken will depend on the type of incident and its effect on the ICS system and the physical process being controlled. A written plan documenting the types of incidents and the response to each type should be prepared. This will provide guidance during times when there might be confusion or stress due to the incident. This plan should include step-by-step actions to be taken by the various organizations. If there are reporting requirements, these should be noted as well as where the report should be made and phone numbers to reduce reporting confusion.

Recovery Actions. The results of the intrusion could be minor, or the intrusion could cause many problems in the ICS. Risk analysis should be conducted to determine the sensitivity of the physical system being controlled to failure modes in the ICS. In each case, step-by-step recovery actions should be documented so that the system can be returned to normal operations as quickly and safely as possible.

During the preparation of the incident response plan, input should be obtained from the various stakeholders including operations, engineering, IT, system support vendors, management, organized labor, legal, and safety. These stakeholders should also review and approve the plan.

6.2.9 Awareness and Training

The security controls that fall within the NIST SP 800-53 Awareness and Training (AT) family provide policy and procedures for ensuring that all users of an information system are provided basic information system security awareness and training materials before authorization to access the system is granted. Personnel training must be monitored and documented.

Supplemental guidance for the AT controls can be found in the following documents:

NIST SP 800-12 provides guidance on security policies and procedures [38].

NIST SP 800-16 provides guidance on security training requirements

NIST SP 800-50 provides guidance on security awareness training [60].

ICS Specific Recommendations and Guidance

For the ICS environment, this must include control system-specific information security awareness and training for specific ICS applications. In addition, an organization must identify, document, and train all personnel having significant ICS roles and responsibilities. Awareness and training must cover the physical process being controlled as well as the ICS.

Security awareness is a critical part of ICS incident prevention, particularly when it comes to social engineering threats. Social engineering is a technique used to manipulate individuals into giving away private information, such as passwords. This information can then be used to compromise otherwise secure systems.

Implementing an ICS security program may bring changes to the way in which personnel access computer programs, applications, and the computer desktop itself. Organizations should design effective training programs and communication vehicles to help employees understand why new access and control methods are required, ideas they can use to reduce risks, and the impact on the organization if control methods are not incorporated. Training programs also demonstrate management's commitment to, and the value of, a cyber security program. Feedback from staff exposed to this type of training can be a valuable source of input for refining the charter and scope of the security program.

6.3 Technical Controls

Technical controls are the security countermeasures for an ICS that are primarily implemented and executed by the system through mechanisms contained in the hardware, software, or firmware components of the system. As discussed in detail in the following subsections, NIST SP 800-53 defines four families of controls within the Technical controls class:

Identification and Authentication (IA): the process of verifying the identity of a user, process, or device, through the use of specific credentials (e.g., passwords, tokens, biometrics), as a prerequisite for granting access to resources in an IT system.

Access Control (AC): the process of granting or denying specific requests for obtaining and using information and related information processing services for physical access to areas within the information system environment.

Audit and Accountability (AU): independent review and examination of records and activities to assess the adequacy of system controls, to ensure compliance with established policies and operational procedures, and to recommend necessary changes in controls, policies, or procedures.

System and Communications Protection (SC): mechanisms for protecting both system and data transmission components.

These technical controls are discussed in more detail in the sections to follow. ICS specific recommendations and guidance, if available, is provided in an outlined box for each section.

Additional ICS specific guidance pertaining to technical controls can be found in ISA TR99.00.01 [33] and the EPRI report: *Supervisory Control and Data Acquisition (SCADA) Systems Security Guide* [61].

6.3.1 Identification and Authentication

Authentication describes the process of positively identifying potential network users, hosts, applications, services, and resources using a combination of identification factors or credentials. The result of this authentication process then becomes the basis for permitting or denying further actions (e.g., when an automatic teller machine asks for a PIN). Based on the authentication determination, the system may or may not allow the potential user access to its resources. Authorization is the process of determining who and what should be allowed to have access to a particular resource; access control is the mechanism for enforcing authorization. Access control is described in Section 6.3.2.

There are several possible factors for determining the authenticity of a person, device, or system, including something you know, something you have or something you are. For example, authentication could be based on something known (e.g., PIN number or password), something possessed (e.g., key, dongle, smart card), something you are such as a biological characteristic (e.g., fingerprint, retinal signature), a location (e.g., Global Positioning System [GPS] location access), the time a request is made, or a combination of these attributes. In general, the more factors that are used in the authentication process, the more robust the process will be. When two or more factors are used, the process is known generically as *multi-factor authentication*.

The security controls that fall within the NIST SP 800-53 Identification and Authentication (IA) family provide policy and guidance for the identification and authentication of users of and devices within the information system. These include controls to manage identifiers and authenticators within each technology used (e.g., tokens, certificates, biometrics, passwords, key cards).

Supplemental guidance for the IA controls can be found in the following documents:

NIST SP 800-12 provides guidance on security policies and procedures [38].

NIST SP 800-63 provides guidance on remote electronic authentication [52].

NIST SP 800-73 provides guidance on interfaces for personal identity verification [48].

NIST SP 800-76 provides guidance on biometrics for personal identity verification [49].

ICS Specific Recommendations and Guidance

Computer systems in ICS environments typically rely on traditional passwords for authentication. Control system suppliers often supply systems with default passwords. These passwords are factory set and are often easy to guess or are changed infrequently, which creates additional security risks. Also, protocols currently used in ICS environments generally have inadequate or no network service authentication. There are now several forms of authentication available in addition to traditional password techniques being used with ICS. Some of these, including password authentication, are presented in the following sections with discussions regarding their use with ICS.

6.3.1.1 Password Authentication

Password authentication technologies determine authenticity based on testing for something the device or human requesting access should know, such as a PIN number or password. Password authentication schemes are thought of as the simplest and most common forms of authentication.

Password vulnerabilities can be reduced by using an active password checker that prohibits weak, recently used, or commonly used passwords. Another weakness is the ease of third-party eavesdropping. Passwords typed at a keypad or keyboard are easily observed or recorded, especially in areas where adversaries could plant tiny wireless cameras or keystroke loggers. Network service authentication often transmits passwords as plaintext (unencrypted), allowing any network capture tool to expose the passwords.

ICS Specific Recommendations and Guidance

One problem with passwords unique to the ICS environment is that a user's ability to recall and enter a password may be impacted by the stress of the moment. During a major crisis when human intervention is critically required to control the process, an operator may panic and have difficulty remembering or entering the password and either be locked out completely or be delayed in responding to the event. Biometric identifiers may have similar drawbacks. Organizations should carefully consider the security needs and the potential ramifications of the use of authentication mechanisms on these critical systems. In situations where the ICS cannot support, or the organization determines it is not advisable (e.g., performance, safety, or reliability are adversely impacted), to implement authentication mechanisms in an ICS, the organization uses compensating controls, such as rigorous physical security controls to provide an equivalent security capability or level of protection for the ICS. This guidance also applies to the use of session lock and session termination in an ICS.

Some ICS operating systems make setting secure passwords difficult, as the password size is very small and the system allows only group passwords at each level of access, not individual passwords. Some industrial (and Internet) protocols transmit passwords in plaintext, making them susceptible to interception. In cases where this practice cannot be avoided, it is important that users have different (and unrelated) passwords for use with encrypted and non-encrypted protocols.

The following are general recommendations and considerations with regards to the use of passwords.

The length, strength, and complexity of passwords should balance security and operational ease of access within the capabilities of the software and underlying OS.

Passwords should have appropriate length and complexity for the required security. In particular, they should not be able to be found in a dictionary or contain predictable sequences of numbers or letters.

Passwords should be used with care on operator interface devices such as control consoles on critical processes. Using passwords on these consoles could introduce potential safety issues if operators are locked out or delayed access during critical events. Physical security should supplement operator control consoles when password protection is not feasible.

The keeper of master passwords should be a trusted employee, available during emergencies. Any copies of the master passwords must be stored in a very secure location with limited access.

The passwords of privileged users (such as network technicians, electrical or electronics technicians and management, and network designers/operators) should be most secure and be changed frequently. Authority to change master passwords should be limited to trusted employees. A password audit record, especially for master passwords, should be maintained separately from the control system.

In environments with a high risk of interception or intrusion (such as remote operator interfaces in a facility that lacks local physical security access controls), organizations should consider supplementing password authentication with other forms of authentication such as challenge/response or multi-factor authentication using biometric or physical tokens.

For user authentication purposes, password use is common and generally acceptable for users logging directly into a local device or computer. Passwords should not be sent across any network unless protected by some form of FIPS-approved encryption or salted cryptographic hash specifically designed to prevent replay attacks. It is assumed that the device used to enter a password is connected to the network in a secure manner.

For network service authentication purposes, passwords should be avoided if possible. There are more secure alternatives available, such as challenge/response or public key authentication.

6.3.1.2 Challenge/response Authentication

Challenge/response authentication requires that both the service requester and service provider know a "secret" code in advance. When service is requested, the service provider sends a random number or string as a challenge to the service requester. The service requester uses the secret code to generate a unique response for the service provider. If the response is as expected, it proves that the service requester has access to the "secret" without ever exposing the secret on the network.

Challenge/response authentication addresses the security vulnerabilities of traditional password authentication. When passwords (hashed or plain) are sent across a network, a portion of the actual "secret" itself is being sent. Authentication is performed by giving the secret to the remote device.

6.3.1.3 Physical Token Authentication

Physical or token authentication is similar to password authentication, except that these technologies determine authenticity by testing for secret code or key produced by a device or token the person requesting access has in their possession, such as security tokens or smart cards. Increasingly, private keys are being embedded in physical devices such as USB dongles. Some tokens support single-factor authentication only, so that simply having possession of the token is sufficient to be authenticated. Others support multi-factor authentication that requires knowledge of a PIN or password in addition to possessing the token.

The primary vulnerability that token authentication addresses is easily duplicating a secret code or sharing it with others. It eliminates the all-too-common scenario of a password to a "secure" system being left on the wall next to a PC or operator station. The security token cannot be duplicated without special access to equipment and supplies. A second benefit is that the secret within a physical token can be very large, physically secure, and randomly generated. Because it is embedded in metal or silicon, it does not have the same risks that manually entered passwords do. If a security token is lost or stolen, the authorized user loses access, unlike traditional passwords that can be lost or stolen without notice.

Common forms of physical/token authentication include:

Traditional physical lock and keys

Security cards (e.g., magnetic, smart chip, optical coding)

Radio frequency devices in the form of cards, key fobs, or mounted tags

Dongles with secure encryption keys that attach to the USB, serial, or parallel ports of computers

One-time authentication code generators (e.g., key fobs)

For single-factor authentication, the largest weakness is that physically holding the token means access is granted (e.g., anyone finding a set of lost keys now has access to whatever they open). Physical/token authentication is more secure when combined with a second form of authentication, such as a memorized PIN used along with the token.

ICS Specific Recommendations and Guidance

Multi-factor authentication is an accepted good practice for access to ICS applications from outside the ICS firewall.

Physical/token authentication has the potential for a strong role in ICS environments. An access card or other token can be an effective form of authentication for computer access, as long as the computer is in a secure area (e.g., once the operator has gained access to the room with appropriate secondary authentication, the card alone can be used to enable control actions).

Biometric Authentication

Biometric authentication technologies determine authenticity by determining presumably unique biological characteristics of the human requesting access. Usable biometric features include finger minutiae, facial geometry, retinal and iris signatures, voice patterns, typing patterns, and hand geometry.

Like physical tokens and smart cards, biometric authentication enhances software-only solutions, such as password authentication, by offering an additional authentication factor and removing the human element in memorizing complex secrets. In addition, because biometric characteristics are unique to a given individual, biometric authentication addresses the issues of lost or stolen physical tokens and smart cards.

Noted issues with biometric authentication include:

Distinguishing a real object from a fake (e.g., how to distinguish a real human finger from a silicon-rubber cast of one or a real human voice from a recorded one).

Generating type-I and type-II errors (the probability of rejecting a valid biometric image, and the probability of accepting an invalid biometric image, respectively). Biometric authentication devices should be configured to the lowest crossover between these two probabilities, also known as the crossover error rate.

Handling environmental factors such as temperature and humidity to which some biometric devices are sensitive.

Addressing industrial applications where employees may have on safety glasses and/or gloves and industrial chemicals may impact biometric scanners.

Retraining biometric scanners that occasionally "drift" over time. Human biometric traits may also shift over time, necessitating periodic scanner retraining.

Requiring face-to-face technical support and verification for device training, unlike a password that can be given over a phone or an access card that can be handed out by a receptionist.

Denying needed access to the control system because of a temporary inability of the sensing device to acknowledge a legitimate user.

Being socially acceptable. Users consider some biometric authentication devices more acceptable than others. For example, retinal scans may be considered very low on the scale of acceptability, while thumb print scanners may be considered high on the scale of acceptability. Users of biometric authentication devices will need to take social acceptability for their target group into consideration when selecting among various biometric authentication technologies.

ICS Specific Recommendations and Guidance

Biometric devices make a useful secondary check versus other forms of authentication that can become lost or borrowed. Using biometric authentication in combination with token-based access control or badge-operated employee time clocks increases the security level. A possible application is in a control room that is environmentally controlled and physically secured [33].

6.3.2 Access Control

The security controls that fall within the NIST SP 800-53 Access Control (AC) family provide policies and procedures for specifying the use of system resources by only authorized users, programs, processes, or other systems. This family specifies controls for managing information system accounts, including establishment, activating, modifying, reviewing, disabling, and removing accounts. Controls cover access and flow enforcement issues such as separation of duties, least privilege, unsuccessful login attempts, system use notification, previous logon notification, concurrent session control, session lock, and session termination. There are also controls to address the use of portable and remote devices and personally owned information systems to access the information system as well as the use of remote access capabilities and the implementation of wireless technologies.

Access can take several forms, including viewing, using, and altering specific data or device functions. Supplemental guidance for the AC controls can be found in the following documents:

NIST SP 800-12 provides guidance on security policies and procedures [38].

NIST SP 800-63 provides guidance on remote electronic authentication [52].

NIST SP 800-48 provides guidance on wireless network security with particular emphasis on the IEEE 802.11b and Bluetooth standards [62].

NIST SP 800-97 provides guidance on IEEE 802.11i wireless network security [63].

FIPS 201 requirements for the personal identity verification of federal employees and contractors [64].

NIST SP 800-96 provides guidance on PIV card to reader interoperability [65].

NIST SP 800-73 provides guidance on interfaces for personal identity verification [48].

NIST SP 800-76 provides guidance on biometrics for personal identity verification [49].

NIST SP 800-78 provides guidance on cryptographic algorithms and key sizes for personal identity verification [66].

If the new federal Personal Identity Verification (PIV) is used as an identification token, the access control system should conform to the requirements of FIPS 201 and NIST SP 800-73 and employ either cryptographic verification or biometric verification. When token-based access control employs cryptographic verification, the access control system should conform to the requirements of NIST SP 800-78. When token-based access control employs biometric verification, the access control system should conform to the requirements of NIST SP 800-76.

Access control technologies are filter and blocking technologies designed to direct and regulate the flow of information between devices or systems once authorization has been determined. The following sections present several access control technologies and their use with ICS.

6.3.2.1 Role-based Access Control (RBAC)

RBAC is a technology that has the potential to reduce the complexity and cost of security administration in networks with large numbers of intelligent devices. Under RBAC, security administration is simplified through the use of roles, hierarchies, and constraints to organize user access levels. RBAC reduces costs within an organization because it accepts that employees change roles and responsibilities more frequently than the duties within roles and responsibilities.

ICS Specific Recommendations and Guidance

RBAC can be used to provide a uniform means to manage access to ICS devices while reducing the cost of maintaining individual device access levels and minimizing errors. RBAC should be used to restrict ICS user privileges to only those that are required to perform each person's job (i.e., configuring each role based on the principle of least privilege).

6.3.2.2 Web Servers

Web and Internet technologies are being added to a wide variety of ICS products because they make information more accessible and products more user-friendly and easier to configure remotely. However, they may also add cyber risks and create new security vulnerabilities that need to be addressed.

ICS Specific Recommendations and Guidance

SCADA and historian software vendors typically provide Web servers as a product option so that users outside the control room can access ICS information. In many cases, software components such as ActiveX controls or Java applets must be installed or downloaded onto each client machine accessing the Web server. Some products, such as PLCs and other control devices, are available with embedded Web, FTP, and e-mail servers to make them easier to configure remotely and allow them to generate e-mail notifications and reports when certain conditions occur. When feasible, use HTTPS rather than HTTP, use SFTP or SCP rather than FTP, block inbound FTP and e-mail traffic, etc.

6.3.2.3 Virtual Local Area Network (VLAN)

VLANs divide physical networks into smaller logical networks to increase performance, improve manageability, and simplify network design. VLANs are achieved through configuration of Ethernet switches. Each VLAN consists of a single broadcast domain that isolates traffic from other VLANs. Just as replacing hubs with switches reduces collisions, using VLANs limits the broadcast traffic, as well as allowing logical subnets to span multiple physical locations. There are two categories of VLANs:

  Static, often referred to as port-based, where switch ports are assigned to a VLAN so that it is transparent to the end user

  Dynamic, where an end device negotiates VLAN characteristics with the switch or determines the VLAN based on the IP or hardware addresses.

Although more than one IP subnet may coexist on the same VLAN, the general recommendation is to use a one-to-one relationship between subnets and VLANs. This practice requires the use of a router or multi-layer switch to join multiple VLANs. Many routers and firewalls support tagged frames so that a single physical interface can be used to route between multiple logical networks.

VLANs are not typically deployed to address host or network vulnerabilities in the way that firewalls or IDS are deployed. However, when properly configured, VLANs do allow switches to enforce security policies and segregate traffic at the Ethernet layer. Properly segmented networks can also mitigate the risks of broadcast storms that may result from port scanning or worm activity.

Switches have been susceptible to attacks such as MAC spoofing, table overflows, and attacks against the spanning tree protocols, depending on the device and its configuration. VLAN hopping, the ability for an attack to inject frames to unauthorized ports, has been demonstrated using switch spoofing or double-encapsulated frames. These attacks cannot be conducted remotely and require local physical access to the switch. A variety of features such as MAC address filtering, port-based authentication using IEEE 802.1x, and specific vendor recommended practices can be used to mitigate these attacks, depending on the device and implementation.

ICS Specific Recommendations and Guidance

VLANs have been effectively deployed in ICS networks, with each automation cell assigned to a single VLAN to limit unnecessary traffic flooding and allow network devices on the same VLAN to span multiple switches [33].

6.3.2.4 Dial-up Modems

ICS systems have stringent reliability and availability requirements. When there is a need to troubleshoot and repair, the technical resources may not be physically located at the control room or facility. Therefore, ICS often use modems to enable vendors, system integrators, or control engineers maintaining the system to dial in and diagnose, repair, configure, and perform maintenance on the network or component. While this allows easy access for authorized personnel, if the dial-up modems are not properly secured, they can also provide backdoor entries for unauthorized use.

Dial-up often uses remote control software that gives the remote user powerful (administrative or root) access to the target system. Such software usually has security options that should be carefully reviewed and configured.

ICS Specific Recommendations and Guidance

Consider using callback systems when dial-up modems are installed in an ICS. This ensures that a dialer is an authorized user by having the modem establish the working connection based on the dialer's information and a callback number stored in the ICS approved authorized user list.

Ensure that default passwords have been changed and strong passwords are in place for each modem.

Physically identify modems in use to the control room operators.

Configure remote control software to use unique user names and passwords, strong authentication, encryption if determined appropriate, and audit logs. Use of this software by remote users should be monitored on an almost real-time frequency.

If feasible, disconnect modems when not in use or consider automating this disconnection process by having modems disconnect after being on for a given amount of time. It should be noted that sometimes modem connections are part of the legal support service agreement with the vendor (e.g., 24x7 support with 15 minute response time). Personnel should be aware that disconnecting/removing the modems may require that contracts be renegotiated.

6.3.2.5 Wireless

The use of wireless within an ICS is a risk-based decision that has to be determined by the organization. Generally, wireless LANs should only be deployed where health, safety, environmental, and financial implications are low. NIST SP 800-48 and SP 800-97 provide guidance on wireless network security.

ICS Specific Recommendations and Guidance

Wireless LANs

Prior to installation, a wireless survey should be performed to determine antenna location and strength to minimize exposure of the wireless network. The survey should take into account the fact that attackers can use powerful directional antennas, which extend the effective range of a wireless LAN beyond the expected standard range. Faraday cages and other methods are also available to minimize exposure of the wireless network outside of the designated areas.

Wireless users' access should utilize IEEE 802.1x authentication using a secure authentication protocol (e.g., Extensible Authentication Protocol [EAP] with TLS [EAP-TLS]) that authenticates users via a user certificates or a Remote Authentication Dial In User Service (RADIUS) server.

The wireless access points and data servers for wireless worker devices should be located on an isolated network with documented and minimal (single if possible) connections to the ICS network.

Wireless access points should be configured to have a unique service set identifier (SSID), disable SSID broadcast, and enable MAC filtering at a minimum.

Wireless devices, if being utilized in a Microsoft Windows ICS network, should be configured into a separate organizational unit of the Windows domain.

Wireless device communications should be encrypted and integrity-protected. The encryption must not degrade the operational performance of the end device. Encryption at OSI Layer 2 should be considered, rather than at Layer 3 to reduce encryption latency. The use of hardware accelerators to perform cryptographic functions should also be considered.

For mesh networks, consider the use of broadcast key versus public key management implemented at OSI Layer 2 to maximize performance. Asymmetric cryptography should be used to perform administrative functions, and symmetric encryption should be used to secure each data stream as well as network control traffic. An adaptive routing protocol should be considered if the devices are to be used for wireless mobility. The convergence time of the network should be as fast as possible supporting rapid network recovery in the event of a failure or power loss. The use of a mesh network may provide fault tolerance thru alternate route selection and pre-emptive fail-over of the network.

Wireless field networks

The ISA100[20] Committee is working to establish standards, recommended practices, technical reports, and related information that will define procedures for implementing wireless systems in the automation and control environment with a focus on the field level (e.g., IEEE 802.15.4). Guidance is directed towards those responsible for the complete life cycle including the designing, implementing, on-going maintenance, scalability or managing industrial automation and control systems, and applies to users, system integrators, practitioners, and control systems manufacturers and vendors.

---

[20] Additional information on ISA100 at: http://www.isa.org/isa100

6.3.3 Audit and Accountability

An audit is an independent review and examination of records and activities to assess the adequacy of system controls, to ensure compliance with established policies and operational procedures, and to recommend necessary changes in controls, policies, or procedures. The security controls that fall within the NIST SP 800-53 Audit and Accountability (AU) family provide policies and procedures for generating audit records, their content, capacity, and retention requirements. The controls also provide safeguards to react to problems such as an audit failure or audit log capacity being reached. Audit data should be protected from modification and be designed with non-repudiation capability.

Supplemental guidance for the AU controls can be found in the following documents:

NIST SP 800-12 provides guidance on security policies and procedures [38].

NIST SP 800-61 provides guidance on computer security incident handling and audit log retention [58].

NIST SP 800-92 provides guidance on log management (including audit logs) [67]

ICS Specific Recommendations and Guidance

It is necessary to determine that the system is performing as intended. Periodic audits of the ICS should be performed to validate the following items:

The security controls present during system validation testing (e.g., factory acceptance testing and site acceptance testing) are still installed and operating correctly in the production system.

The production system is free from security compromises and provides information on the nature and extent of compromises as feasible, should they occur.

The management of change program is being rigorously followed with an audit trail of reviews and approvals for all changes.

The results from each periodic audit should be expressed in the form of performance against a set of predefined and appropriate metrics to display security performance and security trends. Security performance metrics should be sent to the appropriate stakeholders, along with a view of security performance trends.

Traditionally, the primary basis for audit in IT systems has been recordkeeping. Using appropriate tools within an ICS environment requires extensive knowledge from an IT professional familiar with the ICS, critical production and safety implications for the facility. Many of the process control devices that are integrated into the ICS have been installed for many years and do not have the capability to provide the audit records described in this section. Therefore, the applicability of these more modern tools for auditing system and network activity is dependent upon the capabilities of the components in the ICS.

The critical tasks in managing a network in an ICS environment are ensuring reliability and availability to support safe and efficient operation. In regulated industries, regulatory compliance can add complexity to security and authentication management, registry and installation integrity management, and all functions that can augment an installation and operational qualification exercise. Diligent use of auditing and log management tools can provide valuable assistance in maintaining and proving the integrity of the ICS from installation through the system life cycle. The value of these tools in this environment can be calculated by the effort required to re-qualify or otherwise retest the ICS where the integrity due to attack, accident, or error is in question. The system should provide reliable, synchronized time stamps in support of the audit tools.

Monitoring of sensors, logs, IDS, antivirus, patch management, policy management software, and other security mechanisms should be done on a real-time basis where feasible. A first-line monitoring service would receive alarms, do rapid initial problem determination and take action to alert appropriate facility personnel to intervene.

System auditing utilities should be incorporated into new and existing ICS projects. These auditing utilities should be tested (e.g., off-line on a comparable ICS) before being deployed on an operational ICS. These tools can provide tangible records of evidence and system integrity. Additionally, active log management utilities may actually flag an attack or event in progress and provide location and tracing information to help respond to the incident [33].

There should be a method for tracing all console activities to a user, either manually (e.g., control room sign in) or automatic (e.g., login at the application and/or OS layer). Policies and procedures for what is logged, how the logs are stored (or printed), how they are protected, who has access to the logs and how/when are they reviewed should be developed. These policies and procedures will vary with the ICS application and platform. Legacy systems typically employ printer loggers, which are reviewed by administrative, operational, and security staff. Logs maintained by the ICS application may be stored at various locations and may or may not be encrypted.

6.3.4   System and Communications Protection

The security controls that fall within the NIST SP 800-53 System and Communications Protection (SC) family provide policy and procedures for protecting systems and data communications components.

Supplemental guidance for the SC controls can be found in the following documents:

NIST SP 800-28 provides guidance on active content and mobile code [68].

NIST SP 800-52 provides guidance on Transport Layer Security (TLS) Implementations [69]

NIST SP 800-56 provides guidance on cryptographic key establishment [70].

NIST SP 800-57 provides guidance on cryptographic key management [71].

NIST SP 800-58 provides guidance on security considerations for VoIP technologies [72].

NIST SP 800-63 provides guidance on remote electronic authentication [52].

NIST SP 800-77 provides guidance on IPsec VPNs [73].

6.3.4.1 Encryption

Encryption is the cryptographic transformation of data (called plaintext) into a form (called ciphertext) that conceals the data's original meaning to prevent it from being known or used. If the transformation is reversible, the corresponding reversal process is called decryption, which is a transformation that restores encrypted data to its original state [74].

ICS Specific Recommendations and Guidance

Before deploying encryption, first determine if encryption is an appropriate solution for the specific ICS application, because authentication and integrity are generally the key security issues for ICS applications. Other cryptographic solutions such as cryptographic hashes should also be considered.

The use of encryption within an ICS environment could introduce communications latency due to the additional time and computing resources required to encrypt, decrypt, and authenticate each message. For ICS, any latency induced from the use of encryption, or any other security technique, must not degrade the operational performance of the end device or system. Encryption at OSI Layer 2 should be considered, rather than at Layer 3 to reduce encryption latency.

In addition, encrypted messages are often larger than unencrypted messages due to one or more of the following:

Additional checksums to reduce errors

Protocols to control the cryptography

Padding (for block ciphers)

Authentication procedures

Other required cryptographic processes.

Cryptography also introduces key management issues. Sound security policies require periodic key changes. This process becomes more difficult as the geographic size of the ICS increases, with extensive SCADA systems being the most severe example. Because site visits to change keys can be costly and slow, it is useful to be able to change keys remotely.

If cryptography is selected, the most effective safeguard is to use a complete cryptographic system approved by the NIST/ Communications Security Establishment (CSE) Cryptographic Module Validation Program (CMVP)[21]. Within this program standards are maintained to ensure that cryptographic systems were studied carefully for weaknesses by a wide range of experts, rather than being developed by a few engineers in a single organization. At a minimum, certification makes it probable that:

Some method (such as counter mode) will be used to ensure that the same message does not generate the same value each time

ICS messages are protected against replay and forging

Key management is secure throughout the life cycle of the key

---

[21] Information on the CMVP can be found on the CMVP web site http://csrc.nist.gov/cryptval/cmvp.htm

The system is using an effective random number generator

The entire system has been implemented securely.

Even then, the technology is only effective if it is an integral part of an effectively enforced information security policy. American Gas Association (AGA) report 12-1 [5] contains an example of such a security policy. While it is directed toward a natural gas SCADA system, many of its policy recommendations could apply to any ICS.

For an ICS, encryption can be deployed as part of a comprehensive, enforced security policy. Organizations should select cryptographic protection based on a risk assessment and the identified value of the information being protected and ICS operating constraints. Specifically, a cryptographic key should be long enough so that guessing it or determining it through analysis takes more effort, time, and cost than the value of the protected asset.

The encryption hardware should be protected from physical tampering and uncontrolled electronic connections. Assuming cryptography is the appropriate solution, organizations should select cryptographic protection with remote key management if the units being protected are so numerous or geographically dispersed that changing keys is difficult or expensive. [33]

6.3.4.2 Virtual Private Network (VPN)

One method of encrypting communication data is through a VPN, which is a private network that operates as an overlay on a public infrastructure, so that the private network can function across a public network. The most common types of VPN technologies implemented today are:

Internet Protocol Security (IPsec). IPsec is a set of standards defined by IETF to govern the secure communications of data across public networks at the IP layer. IPsec is included in many current operating systems. The intent of the standards is to guarantee interoperability across vendor platforms; however, the reality is that the determination of interoperability of multi-vendor implementations depends on specific implementation testing conducted by the end-user organization. IPsec supports two encryption modes: transport and tunnel. Transport mode encrypts only the data portion (payload) of each packet, but leaves the header untouched. The more secure tunnel mode adds a new header to each packet and encrypts both the original header and the payload. On the receiving side, an IPsec-compliant device decrypts each packet. The protocol has been continually enhanced to address specific requirements, such as extensions to the protocol to address individual user authentication and NAT device transversal. These extensions are typically vendor-specific and can lead to interoperability issues primarily in host-to-security gateway environments. NIST SP 800-77 provides guidance on IPsec VPNs.

Secure Sockets Layer (SSL). SSL provides a secure channel between two machines that encrypts the contents of each packet. The IETF made slight modifications to the SSL version 3 protocol and created a new protocol called Transport Layer Security (TLS). The terms "SSL" and "TLS" are often used interchangeably, and this document generically uses the SSL terminology. SSL is most often recognized for securing HTTP traffic; this protocol implementation is known as HTTP Secure (HTTPS). However, SSL is not limited to HTTP traffic; it can be used to secure many different application layer programs. SSL-based VPN products have gained acceptance because of the market for "clientless" VPN products. These products use standard Web browsers as clients, which have built-in SSL support. The "clientless" term means that there is no need to install or configure third-party VPN "client" software on users' systems. NIST SP 800-52 provides guidance on SSL configuration.

Secure Shell (SSH). SSH is a command interface and protocol for securely gaining access to a remote computer. It is widely used by network administrators to remotely control Web servers and other types of servers. The latest version, SSH2, is a proposed set of standards from the IETF. Typically, SSH is deployed as a secure alternative to a telnet application. SSH is included in most UNIX distributions, and is typically added to other platforms through a third-party package.

ICS Specific Recommendations and Guidance

VPNs are most often used in the ICS environment to provide secure access from an untrusted network to the ICS control network. Untrusted networks can range from the Internet to the corporate LAN. Properly configured, VPNs can greatly restrict access to and from control system host computers and controllers, thereby improving security. They can also potentially improve control network responsiveness by removing unauthorized non-essential traffic from the intermediary network. VPN devices used to protect control systems should be thoroughly tested to verify that the VPN technology is compatible with the application and implementation of the VPN devices does not unacceptably affect network traffic characteristics [33].

Appendix A—Acronyms and Abbreviations

Selected acronyms and abbreviations used in the *Guide to Industrial Control Systems (ICS) Security* are defined below.

AC	Alternating Current
ACL	Access Control List
AGA	American Gas Association
API	American Petroleum Institute
ARP	Address Resolution Protocol
BCP	Business Continuity Plan
CIDX	Chemical Industry Data Exchange
CIGRE	International Council on Large Electric Systems
CIP	Critical Infrastructure Protection
CMVP	Cryptographic Module Validation Program
COTS	Commercial Off-the-Shelf
CPNI	Centre for the Protection of National Infrastructure
CPU	Central Processing Unit
CSE	Communications Security Establishment
CSRC	Computer Security Resource Center
CSSC	Control System Security Center
CVE	Common Vulnerabilities and Exposures
DCOM	Distributed Component Object Model
DCS	Distributed Control System(s)
DETL	Distributed Energy Technology Laboratory
DHS	Department of Homeland Security
DMZ	Demilitarized Zone
DNP	Distributed Network Protocol
DNS	Domain Name System
DOE	Department of Energy
DoS	Denial of Service
DRP	Disaster Recovery Plan
EAP	Extensible Authentication Protocol
EMS	Energy Management System
EPRI	Electric Power Research Institute
ERP	Enterprise Resource Planning
FIPS	Federal Information Processing Standards
FISMA	Federal Information Security Management Act
FTP File	Transfer Protocol
GAO	Government Accountability Office
GPS	Global Positioning System
HMI Human-Machine	Interface
HSPD	Homeland Security Presidential Directive

HTTP	Hypertext Transfer Protocol
HTTPS	Hypertext Transfer Protocol Secure
HVAC	Heating, Ventilation, and Air Conditioning

I/O Input/Output	
I3P	Institute for Information Infrastructure Protection
IAONA	Industrial Automation Open Networking Association
ICMP	Internet Control Message Protocol
ICS	Industrial Control System(s)
IDS	Intrusion Detection System
IEC International	Electrotechnical Commission
IED	Intelligent Electronic Device
IEEE	Institute of Electrical and Electronics Engineers
IETF	Internet Engineering Task Force
IGMP	Internet Group Management Protocol
INL	Idaho National Laboratory
IP Internet	Protocol
IPS	Intrusion Prevention System
IPsec	Internet Protocol Security
ISA	The Instrumentation Systems and Automation Society
ISID	Industrial Security Incident Database
ISO	International Organization for Standardization
IT Information	Technology
ITL	Information Technology Laboratory

LAN Local	Area Network

MAC	Media Access Control
MES Manufacturing	Execution System
MIB Management	Information Base
MTU	Master Terminal Unit (also Master Telemetry Unit)

NAT	Network Address Translation
NCSD	National Cyber Security Division
NERC	North American Electric Reliability Council
NFS	Network File System
NIC	Network Interface Card
NISCC	National Infrastructure Security Coordination Centre
NIST	National Institute of Standards and Technology
NSTB	National SCADA Testbed

OLE	Object Linking and Embedding
OMB	Office of Management and Budget
OPC	OLE for Process Control
OS Operating	System
OSI	Open Systems Interconnection

PCSF	Process Control System Forum
PDA	Personal Digital Assistant

PIN	Personal Identification Number
PID	Proportional – Integral - Derivative
PIV	Personal Identity Verification
PLC	Programmable Logic Controller
PP Protection	Profile
PPP	Point-to-Point Protocol
R&D	Research and Development
RADIUS	Remote Authentication Dial In User Service
RBAC	Role-Based Access Control
RFC	Request for Comments
RMA	Reliability, Maintainability, and Availability
RPC	Remote Procedure Call
RPO	Recovery Point Objective
RTO	Recovery Time Objective
RTU	Remote Terminal Unit (also Remote Telemetry Unit)
SC	Security Category
SCADA Supervisory	Control and Data Acquisition
SCP	Secure Copy
SFTP	Secure File Transfer Protocol
SIS	Safety Instrumented System
SMTP	Simple Mail Transfer Protocol
SNL	Sandia National Laboratories
SNMP	Simple Network Management Protocol
SP Special	Publication
SPP-ICS	System Protection Profile for Industrial Control Systems
SQL	Structured Query Language
SSH	Secure Shell
SSID	Service Set Identifier
SSL	Secure Sockets Layer
TCP	Transmission Control Protocol
TCP/IP	Transmission Control Protocol/Internet Protocol
TFTP	Trivial File Transfer Protocol
TLS	Transport Layer Security
UDP	User Datagram Protocol
UPS	Uninterruptible Power Supply
US-CERT	United States Computer Emergency Readiness Team
USB	Universal Serial Bus
VFD	Variable Frequency Drive
VLAN	Virtual Local Area Network
VPN	Virtual Private Network
WAN	Wide Area Network
XML	Extensible Markup Language

Appendix B—Glossary of Terms

Selected terms used in the *Guide to Industrial Control Systems (ICS) Security* are defined below. Source References for certain definitions are listed at the end of this appendix.

Alternating Current Drive	Synonymous with Variable Frequency Drive (VFD). [28]
Access Control List (ACL)	A mechanism that implements access control for a system resource by enumerating the identities of the system entities that are permitted to access the resources. [1]
Accreditation	The official management decision given by a senior agency official to authorize operation of an information system and to explicitly accept the risk to agency operations (including mission, functions, image, or reputation), agency assets, or individuals, based on the implementation of an agreed-upon set of security controls. [11]
Actuator	A pneumatic, hydraulic, or electrically powered device that supplies force and motion so as to position a valve's closure member at or between the open or closed position. [22]
Alarm	A device or function that signals the existence of an abnormal condition by making an audible or visible discrete change, or both, so as to attract attention to that condition. [20]
Antivirus Tools	Software products and technology used to detect malicious code, prevent it from infecting a system, and remove malicious code that has infected the system.
Application Server	A computer responsible for hosting applications to user workstations. [28]
Attack	An attempt to gain unauthorized access to system services, resources, or information, or an attempt to compromise system integrity, availability, or confidentiality. [2]
Authentication	Verifying the identity of a user, process, or device, often as a prerequisite to allowing access to resources in an information system. [11]
Authorization	The right or a permission that is granted to a system entity to access a system resource. [1]
Backdoor	An undocumented way of gaining access to a computer system. A backdoor is a potential security risk.
Batch Process	A process that leads to the production of finite quantities of material by subjecting quantities of input materials to an ordered set of processing activities over a finite time using one or more pieces of equipment. [24]
Broadcast	Transmission to all devices in a network without any acknowledgment by the receivers. [18]
Buffer Overflow	A condition at an interface under which more input can be placed into a buffer or data holding area than the capacity allocated, overwriting other information. Adversaries exploit such a condition to crash a system or to insert specially crafted code that allows them to gain control of the system. [6]

Certification A comprehensive assessment of the management, operational, and technical security controls in an information system, made in support of security accreditation, to determine the extent to which the controls are implemented correctly, operating as intended, and producing the desired outcome with respect to meeting the security requirements for the system.[9]

Clear Text Information that is not encrypted.

Confidentiality Preserving authorized restrictions on information access and disclosure, including means for protecting personal privacy and proprietary information.[11]

Configuration (of a system or device) Step in system design; for example, selecting functional units, assigning their locations, and defining their interconnections.[17]

Configuration Control Process for controlling modifications to hardware, firmware, software, and documentation to ensure the information system is protected against improper modifications before, during, and after system implementation.[2]

Continuous Process A process that operates on the basis of continuous flow, as opposed to batch, intermittent, or sequenced operations.

Control Algorithm A mathematical representation of the control action to be performed.[19]

Control Center An equipment structure or group of structures from which a process is measured, controlled, and/or monitored.[21]

Control Loop A combination of field devices and control functions arranged so that a control variable is compared to a set point and returns to the process in the form of a manipulated variable.

Control Network Those networks of an enterprise typically connected to equipment that controls physical processes and that is time or safety critical. The control network can be subdivided into zones, and there can be multiple separate control networks within one enterprise and site.[13]

Control Server A server that hosts the supervisory control system, typically a commercially available application for DCS or SCADA system.[28]

Control System A system in which deliberate guidance or manipulation is used to achieve a prescribed value for a variable. Control systems include SCADA, DCS, PLCs and other types of industrial measurement and control systems.

Controlled Variable The variable that the control system attempts to keep at the set point value. The set point may be constant or variable.[19]

Controller A device or program that operates automatically to regulate a controlled variable.[21]

Cycle Time The time, usually expressed in seconds, for a controller to complete one control loop where sensor signals are read into memory, control algorithms are executed, and corresponding control signals are transmitted to actuators that create changes the process resulting in new sensor signals.[19]

Database A repository of information that usually holds plantwide information including process data, recipes, personnel data, and financial data.[28]

Data Historian A centralized database supporting data analysis using statistical process control techniques.

DC Servo Drive A type of drive that works specifically with servo motors. It transmits commands to the motor and receives feedback from the servo motor resolver or encoder.[28]

Denial of Service (DoS)	The prevention of authorized access to a system resource or the delaying of system operations and functions. [1]
Diagnostics	Information concerning known failure modes and their characteristics. Such information can be used in troubleshooting and failure analysis to help pinpoint the cause of a failure and help define suitable corrective measures. [19]
Disaster Recovery Plan (DRP)	A written plan for processing critical applications in the event of a major hardware or software failure or destruction of facilities. [8]
Discrete Process	A type of process where a specified quantity of material moves as a unit (part or group of parts) between work stations and each unit maintains its unique identity. [19]
Distributed Control System (DCS)	In a control system, refers to control achieved by intelligence that is distributed about the process to be controlled, rather than by a centrally located single unit. [19]
Distributed Plant	A geographically distributed factory that is accessible through the Internet by an enterprise. [28]
Disturbance	An undesired change in a variable being applied to a system that tends to adversely affect the value of a controlled variable. [21]
Domain Controller	A server responsible for managing domain information, such as login identification and passwords. [28]
Encryption	Cryptographic transformation of data (called "plaintext") into a form (called "ciphertext") that conceals the data's original meaning to prevent it from being known or used. If the transformation is reversible, the corresponding reversal process is called "decryption", which is a transformation that restores encrypted data to its original state. [1]
Enterprise	An organization that coordinates the operation of one or more processing sites. [24]
Enterprise Resource Planning (ERP) System	A system that integrates enterprise-wide information including human resources, financials, manufacturing, and distribution as well as connects the organization to its customers and suppliers.
Extensible Markup Language (XML)	A specification for a generic syntax to mark data with simple, human-readable tags, enabling the definition, transmission, validation, and interpretation of data between applications and between organizations.
Fault Tolerant	Of a system, having the built-in capability to provide continued, correct execution of its assigned function in the presence of a hardware and/or software fault.
Field Device	Equipment that is connected to the field side on an ICS. Types of field devices include RTUs, PLCs, actuators, sensors, HMIs, and associated communications.
Field Site	A subsystem that is identified by physical, geographical, or logical segmentation within the ICS. A field site may contain RTUs, PLCs, actuators, sensors, HMIs, and associated communications.
Fieldbus	A digital, serial, multi-drop, two-way data bus or communication path or link between low-level industrial field equipment such as sensors, transducers, actuators, local controllers, and even control room devices. Use of fieldbus technologies eliminates the need of point-to-point wiring between the controller and each device. A protocol is used to define messages over the fieldbus network with each message identifying a particular sensor on the network.

File Transfer Protocol (FTP)	FTP is an Internet standard for transferring files over the Internet. FTP programs and utilities are used to upload and download Web pages, graphics, and other files between local media and a remote server which allows FTP access. [15]
Firewall	An inter-network gateway that restricts data communication traffic to and from one of the connected networks (the one said to be "inside" the firewall) and thus protects that network's system resources against threats from the other network (the one that is said to be "outside" the firewall). [1]
Human-Machine Interface (HMI)	The hardware or software through which an operator interacts with a controller. An HMI can range from a physical control panel with buttons and indicator lights to an industrial PC with a color graphics display running dedicated HMI software. [28]
Identification	The process of verifying the identity of a user, process, or device, usually as a prerequisite for granting access to resources in an IT system. [10]
Incident	An occurrence that actually or potentially jeopardizes the confidentiality, integrity, or availability of an information system or the information the system processes, stores, or transmits or that constitutes a violation or imminent threat of violation of security policies, security procedures, or acceptable use policies. Incidents may be intentional or unintentional. [4]
Input/Output (I/O)	A general term for the equipment that is used to communicate with a computer as well as the data involved in the communications. [19]
Insider	An entity inside the security perimeter that is authorized to access system resources but uses them in a way not approved by those who granted the authorization. [1]
Integrity	Guarding against improper information modification or destruction, and includes ensuring information non-repudiation and authenticity. [11]
Intelligent Electronic Device (IED)	Any device incorporating one or more processors with the capability to receive or send data/control from or to an external source (e.g., electronic multifunction meters, digital relays, controllers). [14]
Internet	The single interconnected world-wide system of commercial, government, educational, and other computer networks that share the set of protocols specified by the Internet Architecture Board (IAB) and the name and address spaces managed by the Internet Corporation for Assigned Names and Numbers (ICANN). [1]
Intrusion Detection System (IDS)	A security service that monitors and analyzes network or system events for the purpose of finding, and providing real-time or near real-time warning of, attempts to access system resources in an unauthorized manner. [1]
Intrusion Prevention System (IPS)	A system that can detect an intrusive activity and can also attempt to stop the activity, ideally before it reaches its targets.
Jitter	The time or phase difference between the data signal and the ideal clock.
Key Logger	A program designed to record which keys are pressed on a computer keyboard used to obtain passwords or encryption keys and thus bypass other security measures.
Light Tower	A device containing a series of indicator lights and an embedded controller used to indicate the state of a process based on an input signal. [28]

Local Area Network (LAN)	A group of computers and other devices dispersed over a relatively limited area and connected by a communications link that enables any device to interact with any other on the network.
Machine Controller	A control system/motion network that electronically synchronizes drives within a machine system instead of relying on synchronization via mechanical linkage.
Maintenance	Any act that either prevents the failure or malfunction of equipment or restores its operating capability. [19]
Malware	Software or firmware intended to perform an unauthorized process that will have adverse impact on the confidentiality, integrity, or availability of an information system. A virus, worm, Trojan horse, or other code-based entity that infects a host. Spyware and some forms of adware are also examples of malicious code (malware). [11]
Management Controls	The security controls (i.e., safeguards or countermeasures) for an information system that focus on the management of risk and the management of information security.[5]
Manipulated Variable	In a process that is intended to regulate some condition, a quantity or a condition that the control alters to initiate a change in the value of the regulated condition. [19]
Manufacturing Execution System (MES)	A system that uses network computing to automate production control and process automation. By downloading recipes and work schedules and uploading production results, a MES bridges the gap between business and plant-floor or process-control systems. [28]
Master Terminal Unit (MTU)	See *SCADA Server.*
Modem	A device used to convert serial digital data from a transmitting terminal to a signal suitable for transmission over a telephone channel to reconvert the transmitted signal to serial digital data for the receiving terminal. [28]
Motion Control Network	The network supporting the control applications that move parts in industrial settings, including sequencing, speed control, point-to-point control, and incremental motion. [19]
Network Interface Card (NIC)	A circuit board or card that is installed in a computer so that it can be connected to a network.
Object Linking and Embedding (OLE) for Process Control (OPC)	A set of open standards developed to promote interoperability between disparate field devices, automation/control, and business systems.
Operating System	An integrated collection of service routines for supervising the sequencing of programs by a computer. An operating system may perform the functions of input/output control, resource scheduling, and data management. It provides application programs with the fundamental commands for controlling the computer. [19]
Operational Controls	The security controls (i.e., safeguards or countermeasures) for an information system that are primarily implemented and executed by people (as opposed to systems). [5]
Password	A string of characters (letters, numbers, and other symbols) used to authenticate an identity or to verify access authorization.

Phishing
Tricking individuals into disclosing sensitive personal information by claiming to be a trustworthy entity in an electronic communication (e.g., internet web sites).

Photo Eye
A light sensitive sensor utilizing photoelectric control that converts a light signal into an electrical signal, ultimately producing a binary signal based on an interruption of a light beam. [28]

Port
The entry or exit point from a computer for connecting communications or peripheral devices. [19]

Port Scanning
Using a program to remotely determine which ports on a system are open (e.g., whether systems allow connections through those ports). [12]

Pressure Regulator
A device used to control the pressure of a gas or liquid. [28]

Pressure Sensor
A sensor system that produces an electrical signal related to the pressure acting on it by its surrounding medium. [28] Pressure sensors can also use differential pressure to obtain level and flow measurements.

Printer
A device that converts digital data to human-readable text on a paper medium. [28]

Process Controller
A proprietary computer system, typically rack-mounted, that processes sensor input, executes control algorithms, and computes actuator outputs. [28]

Programmable Logic Controller (PLC)
A solid-state control system that has a user-programmable memory for storing instructions for the purpose of implementing specific functions such as I/O control, logic, timing, counting, three mode (PID) control, communication, arithmetic, and data and file processing. [19]

Protocol
A set of rules (i.e., formats and procedures) to implement and control some type of association (e.g., communication) between systems. [1]

Protocol Analyzer
A device or software application that enables the user to analyze the performance of network data so as to ensure that the network and its associated hardware/software are operating within network specifications. [19]

Proximity Sensor
A non-contact sensor with the ability to detect the presence of a target within a specified range. [28]

Real-Time
Pertaining to the performance of a computation during the actual time that the related physical process transpires so that the results of the computation can be used to guide the physical process. [28]

Redundant Control Server
A backup to the control server that maintains the current state of the control server at all times. [28]

Relay
An electromechanical device that completes or interrupts an electrical circuit by physically moving conductive contacts. The resultant motion can be coupled to another mechanism such as a valve or breaker. [19]

Remote Access
Access by users (or information systems) communicating external to an information system security perimeter. [11]

Remote Diagnostics
Diagnostics activities conducted by individuals communicating external to an information system security perimeter.

Remote Maintenance
Maintenance activities conducted by individuals communicating external to an information system security perimeter.

Remote Terminal Unit (RTU)
A computer with radio interfacing used in remote situations where communications via wire is unavailable. Usually used to communicate with remote field equipment. PLCs with radio communication capabilities are also used in place of RTUs.

Resource Starvation	A condition where a computer process cannot be supported by available computer resources. Resource starvation can occur due to the lack of computer resources or the existence of multiple processes that are competing for the same computer resources.
Risk	The level of impact on agency operations (including mission, functions, image, or reputation), agency assets, or individuals resulting from the operation of an information system, given the potential impact of a threat and the likelihood of that threat occurring.[7]
Risk Assessment	The process of identifying risks to agency operations (including mission, functions, image, or reputation), agency assets, or individuals by determining the probability of occurrence, the resulting impact, and additional security controls that would mitigate this impact. Part of risk management, synonymous with risk analysis. Incorporates threat and vulnerability analyses.[7]
Risk Management	The process of managing risks to agency operations (including mission, functions, image, or reputation), agency assets, or individuals resulting from the operation of an information system. It includes risk assessment; cost-benefit analysis; the selection, implementation, and assessment of security controls; and the formal authorization to operate the system. The process considers effectiveness, efficiency, and constraints due to laws, directives, policies, or regulations.[7]
Router	A computer that is a gateway between two networks at OSI layer 3 and that relays and directs data packets through that inter-network. The most common form of router operates on IP packets. [1]
Router Flapping	A router that transmits routing updates alternately advertising a destination network first via one route, then via a different route.
Safety Instrumented System (SIS)	A system that is composed of sensors, logic solvers, and final control elements whose purpose is to take the process to a safe state when predetermined conditions are violated. Other terms commonly used include emergency shutdown system (ESS), safety shutdown system (SSD), and safety interlock system (SIS). [23]
SCADA Server	The device that acts as the master in a SCADA system. [28]
Security Audit	Independent review and examination of a system's records and activities to determine the adequacy of system controls, ensure compliance with established security policy and procedures, detect breaches in security services, and recommend any changes that are indicated for countermeasures.[16]
Security Controls	The management, operational, and technical controls (i.e., safeguards or countermeasures) prescribed for an information system to protect the confidentiality, integrity, and availability of the system and its information.[3]
Security Plan	Formal document that provides an overview of the security requirements for the information system and describes the security controls in place or planned for meeting those requirements. [11]
Security Policy	Security policies define the objectives and constraints for the security program. Policies are created at several levels, ranging from organization or corporate policy to specific operational constraints (e.g., remote access). In general, policies provide answers to the questions "what" and "why" without dealing with "how." Policies are normally stated in terms that are technology-independent. [13]
Sensor	A device that produces a voltage or current output that is representative of some physical property being measured (e.g., speed, temperature, flow) [19]

Servo Valve	An actuated valve whose position is controlled using a servo actuator. [28]
Set Point	An input variable that sets the desired value of the controlled variable. This variable may be manually set, automatically set, or programmed. [19]
Simple Network Management Protocol (SNMP)	A standard TCP/IP protocol for network management. Network administrators use SNMP to monitor and map network availability, performance, and error rates. To work with SNMP, network devices utilize a distributed data store called the Management Information Base (MIB). All SNMP-compliant devices contain a MIB which supplies the pertinent attributes of a device. Some attributes are fixed or "hard-coded" in the MIB, while others are dynamic values calculated by agent software running on the device. [15]
Single Loop Controller	A controller that controls a very small process or a critical process. [28]
Social Engineering	An attempt to trick someone into revealing information (e.g., a password) that can be used to attack systems or networks. [12]
Solenoid Valve	A valve actuated by an electric coil. A solenoid valve typically has two states: open and closed. [28]
Spyware	Software that is secretly or surreptitiously installed onto an information system to gather information on individuals or organizations without their knowledge; a type of malicious code. [11]
Statistical Process Control (SPC)	The use of statistical techniques to control the quality of a product or process. [19]
Steady State	A characteristic of a condition, such as value, rate, periodicity, or amplitude, exhibiting only negligible change over an arbitrarily long period of time. [21]
Supervisory Control	A term that is used to imply that the output of a controller or computer program is used as input to other controllers. [19]
Supervisory Control and Data Acquisition (SCADA)	A generic name for a computerized system that is capable of gathering and processing data and applying operational controls over long distances. Typical uses include power transmission and distribution and pipeline systems. SCADA was designed for the unique communication challenges (e.g., delays, data integrity) posed by the various media that must be used, such as phone lines, microwave, and satellite. Usually shared rather than dedicated. [19]
Technical Controls	The security controls (i.e., safeguards or countermeasures) for an information system that are primarily implemented and executed by the information system through mechanisms contained in the hardware, software, or firmware components of the system. [5]
Temperature Sensor	A sensor system that produces an electrical signal related to its temperature and, as a consequence, senses the temperature of its surrounding medium. [28]
Threat	Any circumstance or event with the potential to adversely impact agency operations (including mission, functions, image, or reputation), agency assets, or individuals through an information system via unauthorized access, destruction, disclosure, modification of information, and/or denial of service. [11]
Transmission Control Protocol (TCP)	TCP is one of the main protocols in TCP/IP networks. Whereas the IP protocol deals only with packets, TCP enables two hosts to establish a connection and exchange streams of data. TCP guarantees delivery of data and also guarantees that packets will be delivered in the same order in which they were sent. [15]

Trojan Horse   A computer program that appears to have a useful function, but also has a hidden and potentially malicious function that evades security mechanisms, sometimes by exploiting legitimate authorizations of a system entity that invokes the program. [1]

Unauthorized Access   A person gains logical or physical access without permission to a network, system, application, data, or other resource. [12]

Valve   An in-line device in a fluid-flow system that can interrupt flow, regulate the rate of flow, or divert flow to another branch of the system. [19]

Variable Frequency Drive (VFD)   A type of drive that controls the speed, but not the precise position, of a non-servo, AC motor by varying the frequency of the electricity going to that motor. VFDs are typically used for applications where speed and power are important, but precise positioning is not. [28]

Virtual Private Network (VPN)   A restricted-use, logical (i.e., artificial or simulated) computer network that is constructed from the system resources of a relatively public, physical (i.e., real) network (such as the Internet), often by using encryption (located at hosts or gateways), and often by tunneling links of the virtual network across the real network. [1]

Virus   A hidden, self-replicating section of computer software, usually malicious logic, that propagates by infecting (i.e., inserting a copy of itself into and becoming part of) another program. A virus cannot run by itself; it requires that its host program be run to make the virus active. [1]

Virus Definitions   Predefined signatures for known malware used by antivirus detection algorithms.

Vulnerability   Weakness in an information system, system security procedures, internal controls, or implementation that could be exploited or triggered by a threat source. [11]

Wide Area Network (WAN)   A physical or logical network that provides data communications to a larger number of independent users than are usually served by a local area network (LAN) and that is usually spread over a larger geographic area than that of a LAN. [15]

Wireless Device   A device that can connect to a manufacturing system via radio or infrared waves to typically collect/monitor data, but also in cases to modify control set points. [28]

Workstation   A computer used for tasks such as programming, engineering, and design. [28]

Worm   A computer program that can run independently, can propagate a complete working version of itself onto other hosts on a network, and may consume computer resources destructively. [1]

Source References for Glossary Definitions

[1]   RFC 4949, *Internet Security Glossary, Version 2*, August 2007, http://www.rfc-editor.org/rfc/rfc4949.txt.

[2]   National Information Assurance (IA) Glossary, CNSS Instruction no. 4009, revised June 2006.

[3]   FIPS PUB 199, *Standards for Security Categorization of Federal Information and Information Systems*, February 2004.

[4]   FIPS PUB 200, *Minimum Security Requirements for Federal Information and Information System*, March 2006.

[5]   NIST SP 800-18 Revision 1, *Guide for Developing Security Plans for Federal Information Systems*, February 2006.

[6]   NIST SP 800-28, *Guidelines on Active Content and Mobile Code*, October 2001.

[7]   NIST SP 800-30, *Risk Management Guide for Information Technology Systems*, July 2002.

[8]   NIST SP 800-34, *Contingency Planning Guide for Information Technology Systems*, June 2002.

[9]   NIST SP 800-37, *Guide for Security Certification and Accreditation of Federal Information Systems*, May 2004.

[10] NIST SP 800-47, *Security Guide for Interconnecting Information Technology Systems*, Aug 2002.

[11] NIST SP 800-53 Revision 1, *Recommended Security Controls for Federal Information Systems*, July 2006.

[12] NIST SP 800-61, *Computer Security Incident Handling Guide*, January 2004.

[13] ISA SP99 Glossary.

[14] AGA 12, *Cryptographic Protection of SCADA Communications*.

[15] API 1164, *Pipeline SCADA Security, Second Edition*.

[16] ISO/IEC 7498: Information processing systems – Open System Interconnection – Basic reference Model, Part 2: Security Architecture.

[17] IEC/PAS 62409, Real-time Ethernet for Plant Automation, ed 1.0, (2005-06).

[18] IEC/PAS 62410, Real-time Ethernet SERCOS III, ed. 1.0 (2005-08).

[19] *The Automation, Systems, and Instrumentation Dictionary*, 4th Edition, ISA, 2003.

[20] ANSI/ISA-5.1-2009, *Instrumentation Symbols and Identification*.

[21] ANSI/ISA-51.1-1979 - (R1993) - *Process Instrumentation Terminology*.

[22] ANSI/ISA-75.05.01-2000, *Control Valve Terminology*.

[23] ANSI/ISA-84.00.01, 2004.

[24] ANSI/ISA-88.01-1995 - Batch Control Part 1: Models and Terminology.

[25] Bailey, David, and Wright, Edwin, *Practical SCADA for Industry*, IDC Technologies, 2003.

[26] Boyer, Stuart, *SCADA Supervisory Control and Data Acquisition*, 2nd Edition, ISA, 1999.

[27] Erickson, Kelvin, and Hedrick, John, *Plant Wide Process Control*, Wiley & Sons, 1999.

[28] Falco, Joe, et al., *IT Security for Industrial Control Systems*, NIST IR 6859, 2003, http://www.isd.mel.nist.gov/documents/falco/ITSecurityProcess.pdf.

Appendix C—Current Activities in Industrial Control System Security

This appendix contains abstracts of some of the many activities that are currently addressing ICS cyber security. Please be aware that organization descriptions and related information provided in this appendix has been drawn primarily from the listed organizations' Web sites and from other reliable public sources, but has not been verified. Readers are encouraged to contact the organizations directly for the most up-to-date and complete information.

American Gas Association (AGA) Standard 12, "Cryptographic Protection of SCADA Communications"

Standard 12 Documents:
http://www.awwarf.org/research/TopicsAndProjects/Resources/SpecialReports/2969/

American Gas Association: http://www.aga.org/

The American Gas Association, representing 195 local energy utility organizations that deliver natural gas to more than 56 million homes, businesses, and industries throughout the United States, advocates the interests of its energy utility members and their customers, and provides information and services. The AGA 12 series of documents recommends practices designed to protect SCADA communications against cyber incidents. The recommended practices focus on ensuring the confidentiality of SCADA communications. The document series, "Cryptographic Protection of SCADA Communications", when complete will consist of the following four documents:

AGA 12-1 Background, Policies and Test Plan

AGA 12-2 Retrofit Link Encryption for Asynchronous Serial Communications

AGA 12-3 Protection of Networked Systems

AGA 12-4 Protection Embedded in SCADA Components.

The purpose of the AGA 12 series is to save SCADA system owners' time and effort by recommending a comprehensive system designed specifically to protect SCADA communications using cryptography. The AGA 12 series may be applied to water, wastewater, and electric SCADA-based distribution systems because of their similarities with natural gas systems, however timing requirements may be different. Recommendations included in the series 12 documents may also apply to other ICS. Additional topics planned for future addendums in this series include key management, protection of data at rest, and security policies.

American Petroleum Institute (API) Standard 1164, "Pipeline SCADA Security"

American Petroleum Institute: http://api-ec.api.org/

The American Petroleum Institute represents more than 400 members involved in all aspects of the oil and natural gas industry. API 1164 provides guidance to the operators of oil and natural gas pipeline systems for managing SCADA system integrity and security. The guideline is specifically designed to provide operators with a description of industry practices in SCADA security, and to provide the framework needed to develop sound security practices within the operator's individual organizations. It stresses the importance of operators understanding system vulnerability and risks when reviewing the

SCADA system for possible system improvements. API 1164 provides a means to improve the security of SCADA pipeline operations by:

Listing the processes used to identify and analyze the SCADA system's susceptibility to incidents

Providing a comprehensive list of practices to harden the core architecture

Providing examples of industry recommended practices.

The guideline targets small to medium pipeline operators with limited IT security resources. The guideline is applicable to most SCADA systems, not just oil and natural gas SCADA systems. The appendices of the document include a checklist for assessing a SCADA system and an example of a SCADA control system security plan.

Center for SCADA Security at Sandia National Laboratories (SNL)

http://www.sandia.gov/ccss

The Center for SCADA Security is composed of several test bed facilities, which allow real-world critical infrastructure problems to be modeled, designed, simulated, verified, and validated. These labs are integrated into a research effort focusing on solving current control system security problems and developing next generation control systems. These facilities include the following:

Distributed Energy Technology Laboratory (DETL), which provides a platform to test the control of operational generation and load systems

Network Laboratory, which provides network visualization and wired and wireless network modeling

Cryptographic Research Facility, which supports research and development of encryption for applications in control system networks

Red Team Facility, which provides a suite of tools to attack and analyze control system vulnerabilities

Advanced Information Systems Lab, which is used to research intelligent technologies for development of the infrastructures of the future.

Chemical Sector Cyber Security Program

http://www.chemicalcybersecurity.com/

The Chemical Sector Cyber Security Program is a strategic program of the Chemical Information Technology Center (ChemITC) of the American Chemistry Council. The Chemical Sector Cyber Security Program focuses on risk management and reduction to minimize the potential impact of cyber attacks on business and manufacturing systems.

Chemical Industry Data Exchange (CIDX)

http://www.cidx.org/

"At the end of 2008 CIDX transitioned its standards and operations to the Open Application Group, Inc. (OAGi) and the American Chemistry Council's Chemical Information Technology Center (ChemITC®), and then ceased to exist as a corporation

Under the terms of the agreement, CIDX transfered its Chem eStandards® and other related intellectual property to OAGi. OAGi will create a new Chemical Industry Council to provide ongoing support and maintenance for these work products and contribute chemical industry requirements to the development of the OAGIS standard. Chem eStandards will remain free and OAGi standards will be free.

DHS Control Systems Security Program (CSSP)

http://www.uscert.gov/control_systems/

The goal of the DHS National Cyber Security Division's CSSP is to reduce industrial control system risks within and across all critical infrastructure and key resource sectors by coordinating efforts among federal, state, local, and tribal governments, as well as industrial control systems owners, operators and vendors. The CSSP coordinates activities to reduce the likelihood of success and severity of impact of a cyber attack against critical infrastructure control systems through risk-mitigation activities.

The Industrial Control Systems Cyber Emergency Response Team (ICS-CERT) provides a control system security focus in collaboration with US-CERT to:

Respond to and analyze control systems related incidents

Conduct vulnerability and malware analysis

Provide onsite support for incident response and forensic analysis

Provide situational awareness in the form of actionable intelligence

Coordinate the responsible disclosure of vulnerabilities/mitigations

Share and coordinate vulnerability information and threat analysis through information products and alerts

The ICS-CERT serves as a key component of the Strategy for Securing Control Systems, which outlines a long-term, common vision where effective risk management of control systems security can be realized through successful coordination efforts.

DHS CSSP Recommended Practices

http://www.us-cert.gov/control_systems/practices/

The DHS Control Systems Security Program (CSSP) Recommended Practices site provides a current information resource to help industry understand and prepare for ongoing and emerging control systems cyber security issues, vulnerabilities and mitigation strategies.

The CSSP works with the control systems community to ensure that recommended practices, which are made available, have been vetted by subject-matter experts in industry before being made publicly available in support of this program.

Recommended practices are developed to help users reduce their exposure and susceptibility to cyber attacks. These recommendations are based on understanding the cyber threats, control systems vulnerabilities and attack paths, and control systems engineering.

The practices recommended on this site are focused to increase security awareness and provide security practices that have been recommended by industry to aid in a secure architecture. Additional recommended practices and supporting documents that cover specific issues and associated mitigations will continue to be added.

Electric Power Research Institute (EPRI)

http://www.epri.com/

The Electric Power Research Institute (EPRI) is a nonprofit center for public interest energy and environmental research. EPRI brings together member organizations, the Institute's scientists and engineers, and other leading experts to work collaboratively on solutions to the challenges of electric power. These solutions span nearly every area of power generation, delivery, and use, including health, safety, and environment. EPRI's members represent over 90% of the electricity generated in the United States.

During 2006 and 2007, EPRI developed and executed the PowerSec Program to assess utility cyber security and evaluate the gap between existing and recommended practices. Nine electric power companies (EPUs) participated in this program. Six of those EPUs participated in a project to determine their aggregate security posture. This report presents the results of that project.

The intent of the final report is to provide the EPUs that funded the PowerSec Program with a view of their composite security posture. The project team developed a self-assessment framework to help members to evaluate how their cyber security program compares with their peers and with the NERC Critical Infrastructure Protection (CIP) standards. The team conducted six on-site cyber security assessments and analyzed the results.

This report presents a 'snapshot' of security posture of six EPUs that participated in a security survey during 2006 and 2007. The report presents the survey and its results.

Institute of Electrical and Electronics Engineers, Inc. (IEEE)

http://www.ieee.org

IEEE 1686-2007 – Standard for Substation IED Cyber Security Capabilities. The functions and features to be provided in substation intelligent electronic devices (IEDs) to accommodate critical infrastructure protection programs are defined in this standard. Security regarding the access, operation, configuration, firmware revision, and data retrieval from an IED is addressed in this standard. Communications for the purpose of power system protection (teleprotection) is not addressed. Encryption for the secure transmission of data both within and external to the substation, including supervisory control and data acquisition, is not part of this standard as this is addressed in other efforts."

IEEE P1711 - Trial Use Standard for a Cryptographic Protocol for Cyber Security of Substation Serial Links - This trial use standard defines a cryptographic protocol to provide integrity, and optional confidentiality, for cyber security of serial links. It does not address specific applications or hardware implementations, and is independent of the underlying communications protocol.

Institute for Information Infrastructure Protection (I3P)

http://www.thei3p.org/

The I3P is a consortium of leading national cyber security institutions, including academic research centers, government laboratories, and non-profit organizations. It was founded in September 2001 to help meet a well-documented need for improved research and development (R&D) to protect the nation's information infrastructure against catastrophic failures. The institute's main role is to coordinate a national cyber security R&D program and help build bridges between academia, industry, and government. The I3P continues to work toward identifying and addressing critical research problems in information infrastructure protection and opening information channels between researchers, policymakers, and infrastructure operators. Currently, the I3P does the following:

Fosters collaboration among academia, industry, and government on pressing cyber security problems

Develops, manages, and supports national-scale research projects

Provides research fellowship opportunities to qualified post-doctoral researchers, faculty, and research scientists

Hosts workshops, meetings, and events on cyber security and information infrastructure protection issues

Builds and supports a knowledge base as an online vehicle for sharing and distributing information to I3P members and others working on information security challenges.

Membership in the I3P Consortium is at the institutional level; individuals are not eligible. Membership is open to not-for-profit research and academic institutions actively engaged in research and policy focused on cyber security and information infrastructure protection.

International Electrotechnical Commission (IEC) Technical Committees 65 and 57

http://www.iec.ch/

IEC is a standards organization that prepares and publishes international standards for all electrical, electronic, and related technologies. These standards serve as a basis for creating national standards and as references for drafting international tenders and contracts. IEC's members include manufacturers, providers, distributors, vendors, consumers, users, all levels of governmental agencies, professional societies, trade associations, and standards developers from over 60 countries.

In 2004 the IEC Technical Sub-Committee 65C (Industrial Networks), through its working group WG13 (Cyber Security), started to address security issues - within the IEC 61784 standard – for field buses and other industrial communication networks. Results of this work are outlined in part 4, entitled "Digital data communications for measurement and control – Profiles for secure communications in industrial networks".

TC65 WG10 is working to extend this field level communication to address security standards across common automation networking scenarios. The standard being drafted as a result of this work is IEC 62443, entitled "Security for industrial process measurement and control – Network and system security". It is based on a modular security architecture consisting of requirement sets. These modules are mapped into ICS component and network architecture. The resulting requirements can then be formulated for use as the basis for Requests for Proposals (RFP) for data communication standards, and security audits.

TC 57 is focused on Power Systems Management and Associated Information Exchange and is divided up into a series of working groups. Each working group is comprised of members of national standards committees from the countries that participate in the IEC. Each working group is responsible for the development of standards within its domain. The current working groups are:

WG 3: Telecontrol protocols

WG 10: Power system IED communication and associated data models

WG 13: Energy management system application program interface

WG 14: System interfaces for distribution management

WG 15: Data and communication security

WG 16: Deregulated energy market communications

WG 17: Communications systems for distributed energy resources

WG 18: Hydroelectric power plants – communication for monitoring and control

WG 19: Interoperability within TC 57 in the long term

ISA99 Industrial Automation and Control Systems Security Standards

The ISA99 Committee is establishing standards, recommended practices, technical reports, and related information that will define procedures for implementing electronically secure industrial automation and control systems and security practices and assessing electronic security performance. Guidance is directed toward those responsible for designing, implementing, or managing industrial automation and control systems and shall also apply to users, system integrators, security practitioners, and control system manufacturers and vendors.

The committee's focus is to improve the confidentiality, integrity, and availability of components or systems used for automation or control and provide criteria for procuring and implementing secure control systems. Compliance with the committee's guidance will improve industrial automation and control system electronic security, and will help identify vulnerabilities and address them, thereby reducing the risk of compromising confidential information or causing industrial automation control system degradation or failure. There are several standards in the ISA99 series; some are complete and some are in development. Each will cover a specific aspect or subset of the subject of industrial automation and control systems security. The documents have been broken down into four main categories:

ISA-99.01.xx: General Security Requirements for Industrial Automation and Control Systems: The first set of documents in the ISA99 series contains requirements that span the rest of the documents in the ISA99 series. The documents explain terminology, concepts, and models that apply to the whole series and metrics that can be used to measure the performance of the security program and countermeasures.

ISA-99.02.xx: Security Program Requirements for Industrial Automation and Control Systems: The second set of documents in the ISA99 series concerns the establishment, operation, and certification of security programs and is generally end-user focused. Much of the material in the ISA-99.02.xx set of documents is based on management systems from information technology that has been adapted to industrial automation and control systems.

ISA-99.03.xx: System-Level Technical Requirements for Industrial Automation and Control Systems: The third set of documents in the ISA99 series specifies technical capabilities and requirements for systems used in automation and control. These stem from the security program requirements in the ISA-99.02.xx series, but are focused on the technical requirements needed to meet the security program requirements. The scope of this series is very broad and contains everything from end-user requirements for setting up their industrial networks to vendors combining multiple features into a larger product.

ISA-99.04.xx: Component-Level Technical Requirements for Industrial Automation and Control Systems: The fourth set of documents in the ISA99 series specifies technical capabilities and requirements for individual components used in automation and control. These stem from the system-level technical requirements in the ISA-99.03.xx series, but are focused on the individual components that make up full systems. The components may be things such as embedded devices, network hardware, computers, and software packages.

The ISA99 committee was formed in 1992 and at the time this document was published had produced two technical reports and two standards documents, one of which superseded one of the technical reports. In 2009, IEC TC65/WG10 began working with ISA99 to publish the ISA99 document series internationally.

This resulted in the currently published documents being republished as the IEC 62443 series. All future documents and revisions to ISA99 documents are being reviewed and published both by ISA and IEC.

ISA100 Wireless Systems for Automation

http://www.isa.org/isa100

The ISA100 Committee will establish standards, recommended practices, technical reports, and related information that will define procedures for implementing wireless systems in the automation and control environment with a focus on the field level. Guidance is directed towards those responsible for the complete life cycle including the designing, implementing, on-going maintenance, scalability or managing industrial automation and control systems, and shall apply to users, system integrators, practitioners, and control systems manufacturers and vendors.

ISO/IEC 27002:2005 Security Techniques - Code of Practice for Information Security Management

http://www.iso.org/, http://www.27000.org

ISO/IEC 27002:2005 comprises ISO/IEC 17799:2005 and ISO/IEC 17799:2005/Cor.1:2007. Its technical content is identical to that of ISO/IEC 17799:2005. ISO/IEC 17799:2005/Cor.1:2007 changes the reference number of the standard from 17799 to 27002.

ISO/IEC 27002:2005 establishes guidelines and general principles for initiating, implementing, maintaining, and improving information security management in an organization. The objectives outlined provide general guidance on the commonly accepted goals of information security management. ISO/IEC 27002:2005 contains best practices of control objectives and controls in the following areas of information security management:

Security policy

Organization of information security

Asset management

Human resource security

Physical and environmental security

Communications and operations management

Access control

Information systems acquisition, development and maintenance

Information security incident management

Business continuity management

Compliance.

The control objectives and controls in ISO/IEC 27002:2005 are intended to be implemented to meet the requirements identified by a risk assessment. ISO/IEC 27002:2005 is intended as a common basis and practical guideline for developing organizational security standards and effective security management practices, and to help build confidence in inter-organizational activities.

ISO/IEC 27001:2005 Information technology – Security techniques – Information security management systems – Requirements

ISO/IEC 27001:2005 provides a model for establishing, implementing, operating, monitoring, reviewing, maintaining and improving an Information Security Management System. This standard adopts the "Plan-Do-Check-Act" model. This standard covers all types of organizations and specifies the requirements for an Information Security Management System within the context of the organization's overall business risks. The normative control objectives and controls addressed by this standard include:

Security policy

Organization of information security

Asset management

Human resource security

Physical and environmental security

Communications and operations management

Access control

Information systems acquisition, development and maintenance

Information security incident management

Business continuity management

Compliance.

International Council on Large Electric Systems (CIGRE)

http://www.cigre.org/

The International Council on Large Electric Systems (CIGRE) is a nonprofit international association based in France. It has established several study committees to promote and facilitate the international exchange of knowledge in the electrical industry by identifying recommended practices and developing recommendations. Three of its study committees focus on control systems:

The objectives of the B3 Substations Committee include the adoption of technological advances in equipment and systems to achieve increased reliability and availability.

The C2 System Operation and Control Committee focuses on the technical capabilities needed for the secure and economical operation of existing power systems including control centers and operators.

The D2 Information Systems and Telecommunication for Power Systems Committee monitors emerging technologies in the industry and evaluates their possible impact. In addition, it focuses on the security requirements of the information systems and services of control systems.

LOGIIC – Linking the Oil and Gas Industry to Improve Cyber Security

http://www.cyber.st.dhs.gov/logiic.html

LOGIIC is a unique collaborative forum where government and industry are focusing on cyber security issues for the oil and gas industry that are best addressed collaboratively. The needs of the infrastructure owners and operators are driving the formation of projects, supported by government and independent experts. The forms for future collaboration are currently being established, and new projects will be forthcoming.

National SCADA Test Bed (NSTB)

http://www.inl.gov/scada/

The DOE Office of Electricity Delivery and Energy Reliability (OE) seeks to improve the security and reliability of our Nation's energy delivery systems. OE established the National SCADA Test Bed (NSTB) to help the energy sector and equipment vendors assess control system vulnerabilities and test the security of control systems hardware and software. Working in partnership with the energy sector, the National SCADA Test Bed seeks to:

Identify and mitigate existing vulnerabilities.

Facilitate development of security standards.

Serve as an independent entity to test SCADA systems and related control system technologies.

Identify and promote best cyber security practices.

Increase awareness of control systems security within the energy sector.

Develop advanced control system architectures and technologies that are more secure and robust.

Partners in the NSTB include Idaho National Laboratory, Sandia National Laboratories, Argonne National Laboratory, Pacific Northwest National Laboratory, and the National Institute of Standards and Technology.

NIST 800 Series Security Guidelines

http://csrc.nist.gov/publications/nistpubs/index.html

The NIST Special Publication 800 series of documents on information technology reports on the NIST Information Technology Laboratory (ITL) research, guidance, and outreach efforts in computer security, and its collaborative activities with industry, government, and academic organizations. Focus areas include cryptographic technology and applications, advanced authentication, public key infrastructure, internetworking security, criteria and assurance, and security management and support. In addition to NIST SP 800-82, the following is a listing of some additional 800 series documents that have significant relevance to the ICS security community. These as well as many others are available through the URL listed above.

NIST SP 800-18 Revision 1, *Guide for Developing Security Plans for Federal Information Systems*

NIST SP 800-37, *Guide for Applying the Risk Management Framework to Federal Information Systems: A Security Life Cycle Approach*

NIST SP 800-39, *Managing Information Security Risk: Organization, Mission, and Information System View*

NIST SP 800-40 Version 2, *Creating a Patch and Vulnerability Management Program*

NIST SP 800-41, Revision 1, *Guidelines on Firewalls and Firewall Policy*

NIST SP 800-48, *Wireless Network Security: 802.11, Bluetooth, and Handheld Devices*

NIST SP 800-50, *Building an Information Technology Security Awareness and Training Program*

NIST SP 800-53 Revision 3, *Recommended Security Controls for Federal Information Systems and Organizations*

NIST SP 800-53A, *Guide for Assessing the Security Controls in Federal Information Systems and Organizations, Building Effective Security Assessment Plans*

NIST SP 800-61, *Computer Security Incident Handling Guide*

NIST SP 800-63, *Electronic Authentication Guideline*

NIST SP 800-64, *Security Considerations in the Information System Development Life Cycle*

NIST SP 800-70, *Security Configuration Checklists Program for IT Products—Guidance for Checklists Users and Developers*

NIST SP 800-77, *Guide to IPSec VPNs*

NIST SP 800-83, *Guide to Malware Incident Prevention and Handling*

NIST SP 800-86, *Guide to Integrating Forensic Techniques into Incident Response*

NIST SP 800-88, *Guidelines for Media Sanitization*

NIST SP 800-92, *Guide to Computer Security Log Management*

NIST SP 800-94, *Guide to Intrusion Detection and Prevention Systems (IDPS)*

NIST SP 800-97, *Guide to IEEE 802.11i: Robust Security Networks*

NIST SP 800-100, *Information Security Handbook: A Guide for Managers*

NIST SP 800-111, *Guide to Storage Encryption Technologies for End User Devices*

NIST SP 800-115, *Technical Guide to Information Security Testing and Assessment*

NIST SP 800-123, *Guide to General Server Security*

NIST SP 800-127, *Guide to Securing WiMAX Wireless Communications*

NIST SP 800-128, *Guide for Security Configuration Management of Information Systems*

NIST Industrial Control System Security Project

http://csrc.nist.gov/groups/SMA/fisma/ics/

Because today's ICS are often a combination of legacy systems, often with a planned life span of twenty to thirty years, or a hybrid of legacy systems augmented with newer hardware and software that are interconnected to other systems, it is often difficult or infeasible to apply some of the security controls contained in NIST SP 800-53. Recognizing this problem, NIST has initiated the Industrial Control System Security project in cooperation with the public and private sector ICS community to develop specific guidance on the application of NIST documents, including the security controls in NIST SP 800-53 to ICS. To facilitate the understanding of applying NIST SP 800-53 to ICS, a series of ICS cyber security case studies were developed using actual ICS cyber security incidents. These case histories examine the NIST SP 800-53 ICS controls that were violated or not implemented, and postulate the potential mitigations that may have occurred if the controls had been implemented.

North American Electric Reliability Corporation (NERC)

http://www.nerc.com/

NERC's mission is to improve the reliability and security of the bulk power system in North America. To achieve that, NERC develops and enforces reliability standards; monitors the bulk power system; assesses future adequacy; audits owners, operators, and users for preparedness; and educates and trains industry personnel. NERC is a self-regulatory organization that relies on the diverse and collective expertise of industry participants. As the Electric Reliability Organization, NERC is subject to audit by the U.S. Federal Energy Regulatory Commission and governmental authorities in Canada

NERC has issued a set of cyber security standards to reduce the risk of compromise to electrical generation resources and high-voltage transmission systems above 100kV, also referred to as bulk electric systems. Bulk electric systems include Balancing Authorities, Reliability Coordinators, Interchange Authorities, Transmission Providers, Transmission Owners, Transmission Operators, Generation Owners, Generation Operators, and Load Serving Entities. The cyber security standards include audit measures and levels of non-compliance that can be tied to penalties.

The set of NERC Cyber Security Standards includes the following:

CIP-002 Critical Cyber Asset Identification

CIP-003 Security Management Controls

CIP-004 Personnel and Training

CIP-005 Electronic Security Perimeter(s)

CIP-006 Physical Security of Critical Cyber Assets

CIP-007 Systems Security Management

CIP-008 Incident Reporting and Response Planning

CIP-009 Recovery Plans for Critical Cyber Assets

The standards can be downloaded at: http://www.nerc.com/page.php?cid=2|20

SCADA and Control Systems Procurement Project

http://www.msisac.org/scada/

The SCADA Procurement Project, established in March 2006, is a joint effort among public and private sectors focused on development of common procurement language that can be used by everyone. The goal is for federal, state and local asset owners and regulators to come together using these procurement requirements and to maximize the collective buying power to help ensure that security is integrated into SCADA systems.

Smart Grid Interoperability Panel (SGIP) Cyber Security Working Group (CSWG)

http://collaborate.nist.gov/twiki-sggrid/bin/view/SmartGrid/CyberSecurityCTG

The primary goal of the working group is to develop an overall cyber security strategy for the Smart Grid that includes a risk mitigation strategy to ensure interoperability of solutions across different domains/components of the infrastructure. The cyber security strategy needs to address prevention, detection, response, and recovery. Implementation of a cyber security strategy requires the definition and implementation of an overall cyber security risk assessment process for the Smart Grid.

The working group's effort is documented in NIST IR 7628 *Guidelines for Smart Grid Cyber Security* http://csrc.nist.gov/publications/PubsNISTIRs.html#NIST-IR-7628

Appendix D—Emerging Security Capabilities

This section provides an overview of security capabilities that are available to or being developed in support of the ICS community. There are several security products that are marketed specifically for ICS, while others are general IT security products that are being used with ICS. Many of the products available offer "single point solutions", where a single security product offers multiple levels of protection. In addition to available products, this section also discusses some research and development work towards new products and technologies.

Encryption

Encryption protects the confidentiality of data by encoding the data to ensure that only the intended recipient can decode it. There are some commercially available encryption products designed specifically for ICS applications, as well as general encryption products that support basic serial and Ethernet-based communications.

In addition to these products, the ICS SCADA community is working to develop a standard for implementing the encryption of SCADA communications. The American Gas Association is working to develop a standard, AGA-12, *Cryptographic Protection of SCADA Communications*, to protect SCADA master-slave communication links from a variety of active and passive cyber attacks by developing a set of standards to secure serial communication links using encryption. The AGA effort is broken into four parts, with each addressing different aspects of SCADA communication protection:

AGA 12-1 summarizes cyber security policies, the background of the cyber security problem, and a procedure for testing cryptographic protection systems.

AGA 12-2 is a detailed technical specification for building interoperable cryptographic modules to protect SCADA communications for low-speed legacy SCADA systems and dial-up maintenance ports.

AGA 12-3 will describe how to protect high-speed SCADA communications over networked systems.

AGA 12-4 will describe how to build next-generation SCADA systems with embedded AGA 12 compatible cryptography.

Because of the long life of SCADA systems, a decision was made by AGA to focus initial efforts on the protection of legacy systems. This decision has led to the near completion of parts 1 and 2, while parts 3 and 4 are still in the planning stages.

Firewalls

Firewalls are commonly used to segregate networks to protect and isolate ICS. These implementations use commercially available firewalls that are focused on Internet and corporate application layer protocols and are not equipped to handle ICS protocols. The ICS community is investigating the possibility of adding protocol awareness to filtering devices. Research was performed by an IT security vendor in 2003 to develop a Modbus-based firewall that allows policy decisions to be made on Modbus/TCP header values just as traditional firewalls filter on TCP/UDP ports and IP addresses [75]. There are currently efforts to develop industrial firewalls.

Intrusion Detection and Prevention

Intrusion detection systems (IDS) and intrusion prevention systems (IPS) are being deployed on ICS networks and components to detect well-known cyber attacks. Network IDS products monitor network traffic and use various detection methods, such as comparing portions of the traffic to signatures of known attacks. In contrast, host intrusion detection uses software loaded on a host computer, often with attack signatures, to monitor ongoing events and data on a computer system for possible exploits. IPS products take intrusion detection a step further by automatically acting on detected exploits to attempt to stop them [56].

The required task of a security team to constantly monitor, evaluate, and quickly respond to intrusion detection events is sometimes contracted to a managed security service provider (MSSP). MSSPs have correlation and analysis engines to process and reduce the vast amounts of events logged per day to a small subset that needs to be manually evaluated. There are also correlation and analysis engine products available to large organizations wanting to perform this function in-house. Security information and event management (SIEM) products are used in some organizations to monitor, analyze, and correlate events from IDS and IPS logs, as well as audit logs from other computer systems, applications, infrastructure equipment, and other hardware and software, to look for intrusion attempts.

Current IDS and IPS products are effective in detecting and preventing many well-known Internet attacks, but until recently they have not addressed ICS protocol attacks. IDS and IPS vendors are beginning to develop and incorporate attack signatures for various ICS protocols such as Modbus, DNP, and ICCP. One cooperative effort within the ICS community is developing Snort rules for Modbus TCP, DNP3, and ICCP. Snort is an open source network intrusion detection and prevention system using a rule-driven language to perform signature, protocol, and anomaly-based inspections. The current rule sets, covering Modbus, DNP, and ICCP, are basic, and efforts are underway to expand them. This same industry group is also defining a data dictionary of log entries from various ICS applications. The data dictionary helps cyber security monitoring products and services identify and understand the meaning of security events in ICS application logs using normalized events. The dictionary is still under development. Some commercial IDS and IPS vendors are also offering some ICS protocol signatures. [57].

As with any software added to an ICS component, the addition of host IDS or IPS software could affect system performance. IPSs are commonplace in today's information security industry, but can be very resource intensive. These systems have the ability to automatically reconfigure systems if an intrusion attempt is identified. This automated and fast reaction is designed to prevent successful exploits; however, an automated tool such as this could be used by an adversary to adversely effect the operation on an ICS by shutting down segments of a network or server. False positives can also hinder ICS operation.

Malware/Antivirus Software

Because early malware threats were primarily viruses, the software to detect and remove malware has historically been called "antivirus software", even though it can detect many types of malware. Antivirus software is used to counter the threats of malware by evaluating files on a computer's storage devices (some tools also detect malware in real-time at the network perimeter and/or on the user's workstation) against an inventory of malware signature files. If one of the files on a computer matches the profile of known malware, the malware is removed through a disinfection process so it cannot infect other local files or communicate across a network to infect other files on other computers. There are also techniques available to identify unknown malware "in-the-wild" when a signature file is not yet available.

Many end-users and vendors of ICS are recommending the use of COTS antivirus software with their systems and have even developed installation and configuration guidance based on their own laboratory testing. Some ICS vendors recommend the use of antivirus software with their products, but offer little to no guidance. Some end users and vendors are hesitant to use antivirus software due to fears that its use would cause ICS performance problems or even failure. NIST and Sandia National Laboratories (SNL) are conducting a study and producing a report aimed at helping ICS owners/operators to deploy antivirus software and to minimize and assess performance impacts of workstation and server-based antivirus products. This study has assembled ICS-based antivirus knowledge and serves as a starting point or a secondary resource when installing, configuring, running, and maintaining antivirus software on an ICS [55]. In many cases, performance impacts can be reduced through configuration settings as well as antivirus scanning and maintenance scheduling outside of the antivirus software practices recommended for typical IT systems.

In summary, COTS antivirus software can be used successfully on most ICS components. However, special ICS specific considerations should be taken into account during the selection, installation, configuration, operational, and maintenance procedures. ICS end-users should consult with the ICS vendors regarding the use of antivirus software and can also use the output of the NIST and SNL study as supplemental information.

Vulnerability and Penetration Testing Tools

There are many tools available for performing network vulnerability assessments and penetration tests for typical IT networks; however, the impacts these tools may have on the operation of an ICS should be carefully considered [76]. The additional traffic and exploits used during active vulnerability and penetration testing, combined with the limited resources of many ICS, have been known to cause ICS to malfunction. As guidance in this area, SNL has developed a preferred list of vulnerability and penetration testing techniques for ICS [76]. These are less intrusive methods, passive instead of active, to collect the majority of information that is often queried by automated vulnerability and penetration testing tools. These methods are intended to allow collection of the necessary vulnerability information without the risk of causing a failure while testing.

ICS owners must make the individuals using vulnerability and penetration testing tools aware of the criticality of continuous operation and the risks involved with performing these tests on operational systems. It may be possible to mitigate these risks by performing tests on ICS components such as redundant servers or independent test systems in a laboratory setting. Laboratory tests can be used to screen out test procedures that might harm the operational system. Even with very good configuration management to assure that the test system is highly representative, tests on the actual system are likely to uncover flaws not represented in the laboratory.

Appendix E—Industrial Control Systems in the FISMA Paradigm

In recognition of the importance of information security to the economic and national interests of the United States, the Federal Information Security Management Act (FISMA) [13] was established to require each Federal agency to develop, document, and implement an agency-wide program to provide information security for the information and information systems that support the operations and assets of the agency. The NIST FISMA Implementation Project [14] was established in January 2003 to produce several key security standards and guidelines required by Congressional legislation including:

Standards to categorize information and information systems based on the objectives of providing appropriate levels of information security according to a range of risk levels

Guidelines recommending the types of information and information systems to be included in each category

Minimum information security requirements (i.e., management, operational, and technical controls) for information and information systems in each category.

Key FISMA-related publications include Federal Information Processing Standards (FIPS) 199, FIPS 200, and NIST SPs 800-18, 800-37, 800-39, 800-53, 800-53A, 800-59 and 800-60. NIST has initiated the Industrial Control System Security project[22] in cooperation with the public and private sector ICS community to develop specific guidance on the application of FISMA documents, including the security controls in NIST SP 800-53, to ICS. Below is a listing of NIST FIPS and SPs documenting these standards and guidelines.[23]

FIPS Publication 199: Standards for Security Categorization of Federal Information and Information Systems contains standards to categorize information and information systems based on the objectives of providing appropriate levels of information security according to a range of risk levels [15]. The security categories are based on the potential impact on an organization should certain events occur which jeopardize the information and information systems needed by the organization to accomplish its assigned mission, protect its assets, fulfill its legal responsibilities, maintain its day-to-day functions, and protect individuals. Security categories are to be used in conjunction with vulnerability and threat information in assessing the risk to an organization resulting from the operation of its information systems.

FIPS Publication 200: Minimum Security Requirements for Federal Information and Information Systems specifies minimum security requirements for information and information systems supporting the executive agencies of the Federal government and a risk-based process for selecting the security controls necessary to satisfy the minimum security requirements [16]. The document provides links to NIST SP 800-53 (*Recommended Security Controls for Federal Information Systems and Organizations*), which recommends management, operational, and technical controls needed to protect the confidentiality, integrity, and availability of all Federal information systems that are not national security systems.

NIST SP 800-18: Guide for Developing Security Plans for Information Systems contains guidelines to develop, document, and implement an agency-wide information security program that includes subordinate plans for providing adequate information security for networks, facilities, and systems or groups of information systems [17].

---

[22] The Industrial Control System Security Project Web site is located at: http://csrc.nist.gov/groups/SMA/fisma/ics/
[23] All of these publications are available from the NIST Computer Security Resource Center (CSRC) Web site, located at http://csrc.nist.gov/

NIST SP 800-30: Risk Management Guide for Information Technology Systems has guidelines to develop an agency-wide information security program that includes periodic assessment of the risk and magnitude of the harm that could result from unauthorized access, use disclosure, disruption, modifications, or destruction of information and information systems.

NIST SP 800-37: Guide for the Security Certification and Accreditation of Federal Information Systems provides guidance for applying the Risk Management Framework to federal information systems to include conducting the activities of security categorization, security control selection and implementation, security control assessment, information system authorization, and security control monitoring [20].

NIST SP 800-39: Managing Information Security Risk provides guidance for an integrated, organization-wide program for managing information security risk to organizational operations (i.e., mission, functions, image, and reputation), organizational assets, individuals, other organizations, and the Nation resulting from the operation and use of federal information systems. Special Publication 800-39 provides a structured, yet flexible approach for managing risk that is intentionally broad-based, with the specific details of assessing, responding to, and monitoring risk on an ongoing basis provided by other supporting NIST security standards and guidelines [19].

NIST SP 800-53: Recommended Security Controls for Federal Information Systems and Organizations provides guidelines for selecting and specifying security controls for information systems supporting the executive agencies of the Federal government [21]. The guidelines apply to all components of an information system that process, store, or transmit Federal information with the exception of systems designated as national security systems.

NIST SP 800-53A: Guide for Assessing Security Controls in Federal Information Systems and Organizations, Building Effective Security Assessment Plans provides guidance for conducting periodic testing and evaluation of the effectiveness of information security policies, procedures, and practices (including management, operational, and technical security controls) [22].

NIST SP 800-59: Guideline for Identifying an Information System as a National Security System provides guidelines developed in conjunction with the Department of Defense, including the National Security Agency, for identifying an information system as a national security system [23].

NIST SP 800-60: Guide for Mapping Types of Information and Information Systems to Security Categories presents guidelines that recommend the types of information and information systems to be included in each security category defined in FIPS 199 [24].

NIST SP 800-70: Security Configuration Checklists Program for IT Products: Guidance for Checklists Users and Developers discusses the development of security configuration checklists and option selections that minimize the security risks associated with commercial IT products used within the Federal government [25].[24]

---

[24] More information on this program is available at http://checklists.nist.gov/.

This set of documents provides security standards and guidelines that support an enterprise-wide risk management process. The documents are intended to be an integral part of a Federal agency's overall information security program. The Risk Management Framework, illustrated in Figure E-1, provides a disciplined and structured process that integrates information security and risk management activities into the system development life. NIST SP 800-37 provides guidance applying the Risk Management Framework to federal information systems to include conducting the activities of security categorization,[25] security control selection and implementation, security control assessment, information system authorization,[26] and security control monitoring.

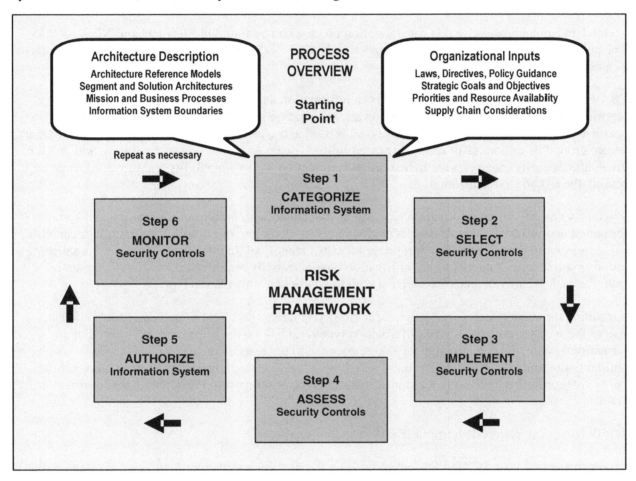

Figure E-1. Risk Management Framework

The following is a chronological listing of the Risk Management Framework activities, a description of each activity, and identification of supporting NIST documents. [26]

Categorize Information System

The first activity in the Risk Management Framework is to categorize the information and information system according to potential impact of loss. For each information type and information system under

---

[25] FIPS 199 provides security categorization guidance for nonnational security systems. CNSS Instruction 1253 provides similar guidance for national security systems.

[26] Security *authorization* is the official management decision given by a senior organizational official to authorize operation of an information system and to explicitly accept the risk to organizational operations and assets, individuals, other organizations, and the Nation based on the implementation of an agreed-upon set of security controls.

consideration, the three FISMA-defined security objectives—confidentiality, integrity, and availability—are associated with one of three levels of potential impact should there be a breach of security. It is important to remember that for an ICS, availability is generally the greatest concern.

The generalized format for expressing the Security Category (SC) is:

SC $_{\text{information type or system}}$ = {(**confidentiality**, *impact*), (**integrity**, *impact*), (**availability**, *impact*)},

where the acceptable values for potential impact are LOW, MODERATE, or HIGH.

The standards and guidance for this categorization process can be found in FIPS 199 and NIST SP 800-60, respectively. NIST is in the process of updating NIST SP 800-60 to provide additional guidance on the categorization of ICS.

FIPS 199 establishes security categories for both information and information systems. The security categories are based on the potential impact on an organization should certain events occur which jeopardize the information and information systems needed by the organization to accomplish its assigned mission, protect its assets, fulfill its legal responsibilities, maintain its day-to-day functions, and protect individuals. Security categories are to be used in conjunction with vulnerability and threat information in assessing the risk to an organization.

The security category of an information type can be associated with both user information and system information and can be applicable to information in either electronic or non-electronic form. It can also be used as input in considering the appropriate security category of an information system. Establishing an appropriate security category of an information type essentially requires determining the potential impact for each security objective associated with the particular information type.

Determining the security category of an information system requires slightly more analysis and must consider the security categories of all information types resident on the information system. For an information system, the potential impact values assigned to the respective security objectives (confidentiality, integrity, availability) are the highest values (i.e., high water mark) from among those security categories that have been determined for each type of information resident on the information system.

The following example is taken from FIPS 199:

A power plant contains a SCADA system controlling the distribution of electric power for a large military installation. The SCADA system contains both real-time sensor data and routine administrative information. The management at the power plant determines that: (i) for the sensor data being acquired by the SCADA system, there is no potential impact from a loss of confidentiality, a high potential impact from a loss of integrity, and a high potential impact from a loss of availability; and (ii) for the administrative information being processed by the system, there is a low potential impact from a loss of confidentiality, a low potential impact from a loss of integrity, and a low potential impact from a loss of availability. The resulting security categories, SC, of these information types are expressed as:

SC sensor data = {(**confidentiality**, NA), (**integrity**, HIGH), (**availability**, HIGH)},

and

SC administrative information = {(**confidentiality**, LOW), (**integrity**, LOW), (**availability**, LOW)}.

The resulting security category of the information system is initially expressed as:

SC SCADA system = {(**confidentiality**, LOW), (**integrity**, HIGH), (**availability**, HIGH)},

representing the high water mark or maximum potential impact values for each security objective from the information types resident on the SCADA system. The management at the power plant chooses to increase the potential impact from a loss of confidentiality from low to moderate, reflecting a more realistic view of the potential impact on the information system should there be a security breach due to the unauthorized disclosure of system-level information or processing functions. The final security category of the information system is expressed as:

SC SCADA system = {(**confidentiality**, MODERATE), (**integrity**, HIGH), (**availability**, HIGH)}.

FIPS 199 specifies that information systems be categorized as low-impact, moderate-impact, or high-impact for the security objectives of confidentiality, integrity, and availability. Possible definitions for low, moderate, and high levels of security based on impact for ICS based on ISA99 are provided in Table E-1. Possible definitions for ICS impact levels based on product produced, industry and security concerns are provided in Table E-2.

Table E-1. Possible Definitions for ICS Impact Levels Based on ISA99

Impact Category	Low-Impact	Moderate-Impact	High-Impact
Injury	Cuts, bruises requiring first aid	Requires hospitalization	Loss of life or limb
Financial Loss	$1,000	$100,000	Millions
Environmental Release	Temporary damage	Lasting damage	Permanent damage, off-site damage
Interruption of Production	Minutes Days Weeks		
Public Image	Temporary damage	Lasting damage	Permanent damage

Table E-2. Possible Definitions for ICS Impact Levels Based on Product Produced, Industry and Security Concerns

Category	Low-Impact	Moderate-Impact	High-Impact
Product Produced	• Non-hazardous materials or products • Non-ingested consumer products	• Some hazardous products or steps during production • High amount of proprietary information	• Critical infrastructure (e.g., electricity) • Hazardous materials • Ingested products
Industry Examples	• Plastic injection molding • Warehouse applications	• Automotive metal industries • Pulp and paper • Semiconductors	• Utilities • Petrochemical • Food and beverage • Pharmaceutical
Security Concerns	• Protection against minor injuries • Ensuring uptime	• Protection against moderate injuries • Ensuring uptime • Capital investment	• Protection against major injuries/loss of life • Ensuring uptime • Capital investment • Trade secrets • Ensuring basic social services • Regulatory compliance

Select Security Controls

This framework activity includes the initial selection of minimum security controls planned or in place to protect the information system based on a set of requirements. FIPS PUB 200 documents a set of minimum-security requirements covering 17 security-related areas with regard to protecting the confidentiality, integrity, and availability of Federal information systems and the information processed, stored, and transmitted by those systems. The security-related areas are:

Access Control (AC)

Awareness and Training (AT)

Audit and Accountability (AU)

Security Assessment and Authorization (CA)

Configuration Management (CM)

Contingency Planning (CP)

Identification and Authentication (IA)

Incident Response (IR)

Maintenance (MA)

Media Protection (MP)

Physical and Environmental Protection (PE)

Planning (PL)

Personnel Security (PS)

Risk Assessment (RA)

System and Services Acquisition (SA)

System and Communications Protection (SC)

System and Information Integrity (SI).

Program Management (PM)

To aid in selecting controls to meet these requirements, NIST SP 800-53 provides fundamental concepts and a process for selection and specification of security controls for an information system. Security controls are organized into classes and families for ease of use in the selection and specification process. Each family name and unique control identifier corresponds to the above listing of minimum-security requirements. The families are divided among three classes: management, operational, and technical. Each security control within a family contains the following information:

Control – describes specific security related activities or actions to be carried out by the organization or the information system. The control selections often contain assignment and selection options for customizing a security control.

Supplemental Guidance – provides additional information related to a specific security control that should be considered when selecting and implementing security controls.

Control Enhancements – provides statements of security capability to add functionality to or increase the strength of a basic control.

Implement Security Controls

This activity involves the implementation of security controls in new or legacy information systems. To help make this process consistent across the Federal government, NIST is currently working to develop security configuration checklists, which are documented sets of instructions for configuring products to pre-defined security baselines [27] (e.g., NIST SP 800-68, *Guidance for Securing Microsoft Windows XP Systems for IT Professionals: A NIST Security Configuration Checklist*).

Assess Security Controls

This activity determines the extent to which the security controls in the information system are effective in their application. NIST SP 800-53A provides guidance for assessing security controls initially selected from NIST SP 800-53 to ensure they are implemented correctly, operating as intended, and producing the desired outcome with respect to meeting the security requirements of the system. To accomplish this, the document provides expectations based on assurance requirements defined in NIST SP 800-53 for characterizing the expectations of security assessments by FIPS 199 impact level. NIST SP 800-53A also supports:

FISMA annual assessments for major information systems

Security certifications as part of formal system certification and accreditation processes

Continuous monitoring of selected security controls

Preparation for an audit

Identification of resource needs to improve the system's security posture

Authorize Information System

This activity results in a management decision to authorize the operation of an information system and to explicitly accept the risk to agency operations, agency assets, or individuals based on the implementation of an agreed-upon set of security controls.

Monitor Security Controls

This activity continuously tracks changes to the information system that may affect security controls and assesses control effectiveness. NIST SP 800-37 provides guidance on continuous monitoring.

Guidance on the Application of Security Controls to ICS

Because today's ICS are often a combination of legacy systems, often with a planned life span of twenty to thirty years, or a hybrid of legacy systems augmented with newer hardware and software that are interconnected to other systems, it is often difficult or infeasible to apply some of the security controls contained in NIST SP 800-53. Recognizing this problem, NIST created the Industrial Control System Security project[27] in cooperation with the public and private sector ICS community to develop specific guidance on the application of the security controls in NIST SP 800-53 to ICS.

While most controls in Appendix F of NIST SP 800-53 are applicable to ICS as written, several controls did require ICS-specific interpretation and/or augmentation by adding one or more of the following to the control:

> ICS Supplemental Guidance provides organizations with additional information on the application of the security controls and control enhancements in Appendix F of NIST SP 800-53 to ICS and the environments in which these specialized systems operate. The Supplemental Guidance also provides information as to why a particular security control or control enhancement may not be applicable in some ICS environments and may be a candidate for tailoring (i.e., the application of scoping guidance and/or compensating controls). ICS Supplemental Guidance does not replace the original Supplemental Guidance in Appendix F of NIST SP 800-53.
>
> ICS Enhancements (one or more) that provide enhancement augmentations to the original control that may be required for some ICS
>
> ICS Enhancement Supplemental Guidance that provides guidance on how the control enhancement applies, or does not apply, in ICS environments.

This ICS-specific guidance is included in NIST SP 800-53, Revision 3, Appendix I: Industrial Control Systems – Security Controls, Enhancements, and Supplemental Guidance. Section 6 of this document also provides initial guidance on how 800-53 security controls apply to ICS. Initial recommendations and guidance, if available, are provided in an outlined box for each section. NIST is planning a December 2011 update to NIST SP 800-53 (NIST SP 800-53, Revision 4), including an update of current security controls, control enhancements, supplemental guidance, as well as tailoring and supplementation guidance, in the area of industrial control systems.

In addition, NIST recommends that ICS owners take advantage of the ability to tailor the initial baselines when it is not possible or feasible to implement specific security controls contained in the baselines. However, all tailoring activity should, as its primary goal, focus on meeting the intent of the original security controls whenever possible or feasible.

In situations where the ICS cannot support, or the organization determines it is not advisable to implement particular security controls or control enhancements in an ICS (e.g., performance, safety, or reliability are adversely impacted), the organization provides a complete and convincing rationale for how the selected compensating controls provide an equivalent security capability or level of protection for the ICS and why the related baseline security controls could not be employed.

If the ICS cannot support the use of automated mechanisms, the organization employs nonautomated mechanisms or procedures as compensating controls in accordance with the general tailoring guidance in Section 3.3 of NIST SP 800-53.

Compensating controls are not exceptions or waivers to the baseline controls; rather, they are alternative safeguards and countermeasures employed within the ICS that accomplish the intent of the original

---

[27] The Industrial Control System Security Project Web site is located at: http://csrc.nist.gov/groups/SMA/fisma/ics/

security controls that could not be effectively employed. Organizational decisions on the use of compensating controls are documented in the security plan for the ICS.

To facilitate the understanding of applying NIST SP 800-53 to ICS, a series of ICS cyber security case histories using actual ICS cyber security incidents, has been developed. These case histories examine the NIST SP 800-53 ICS controls that were violated or not implemented, and postulate the potential mitigations that may have occurred if the controls had been implemented.   Please visit the project website for the current releases of these documents.

Appendix F—References

[1] Frazer, Roy, *Process Measurement and Control – Introduction to Sensors, Communication Adjustment, and Control*, Prentice-Hall, Inc., 2001.

[2] Falco, Joe, et al., *IT Security for Industrial Control Systems*, NIST IR 6859, 2003, http://www.isd.mel.nist.gov/documents/falco/ITSecurityProcess.pdf.

[3] Bailey, David, and Wright, Edwin, *Practical SCADA for Industry*, IDC Technologies, 2003.

[4] Boyer, Stuart, *SCADA Supervisory Control and Data Acquisition*, 2nd Edition, ISA, 1999.

[5] AGA-12, Cryptographic Protection of SCADA Communications, Part 1: Background, Policies and Test Plan, September, 2005, http://www.awwarf.org/research/TopicsAndProjects/Resources/SpecialReports/2969/AGAPart1.pdf

[6] Erickson, Kelvin, and Hedrick, John, *Plant Wide Process Control*, Wiley & Sons, 1999.

[7] Berge, Jonas, *Fieldbuses for Process Control: Engineering, Operation, and Maintenance*, ISA, 2002.

[8] Peerenboom, James, *Analyzing Infrastructure Interdependencies: Overview of Concepts and Terminology*, Argonne National Laboratory, http://www.computer.org/portal/web/csdl/doi/10.1109/HICSS.2007.78.

[9] Rinaldi, et al., *Identifying, Understanding, and Analyzing Critical Infrastructure Interdependencies*, IEEE Control Systems Magazine, 2001, http://www.ce.cmu.edu/~hsm/im2004/readings/CII-Rinaldi.pdf.

[10] GAO-04-354, *Critical Infrastructure Protection: Challenges and Efforts to Secure Control Systems*, U.S. GAO, 2004, http://www.gao.gov/new.items/d04354.pdf.

[11] Weiss, Joseph, "Current Status of Cyber Security of Control Systems", Presentation to Georgia Tech Protective Relay Conference, May 8, 2003.

[12] Keeney, Michelle et al., *Insider Threat Study: Computer System Sabotage in Critical Infrastructure Sectors*, United States Secret Service and Carnegie Mellon Software Institute, 2005, http://www.cert.org/archive/pdf/insidercross051105.pdf.

[13] Federal Information Security Management Act of 2002, Section 301: Information Security, http://csrc.nist.gov/drivers/documents/FISMA-final.pdf.

[14] Federal Information Security Management Act Implementation Project, http://csrc.nist.gov/groups/SMA/fisma/index.html.

[15] Federal Information Processing Standards Publication: FIPS 199, *Standards for Security Categorization of Federal Information Systems*, NIST, 2004, http://csrc.nist.gov/publications/fips/fips199/FIPS-PUB-199-final.pdf.

[16] Federal Information Processing Standards Publication: FIPS 200, *Minimum Security Requirements for Federal Information Systems*, NIST, 2006, http://csrc.nist.gov/publications/fips/fips200/FIPS-200-final-march.pdf.

[17] Swanson, Marianne, et al., NIST SP 800-18, *Guide for Developing Security Plans for Federal Information Systems,* Revision 1, 2006, http://csrc.nist.gov/publications/PubsSPs.html

[18] Swanson, Marianne, NIST SP 800-26, *Security Self-Assessment Guide for Information Technology Systems*, 2001, http://csrc.nist.gov/publications/PubsSPs.html.

[19] Ross, Ron, et al., NIST SP 800-39, *Managing Information Security Risk*, 2011, http://csrc.nist.gov/publications/PubsSPs.html.

[20] Ross, Ron, et al., NIST SP 800-37, Revision 1, *Guide for Applying the Risk Management Framework to Federal Information Systems*, 2010, http://csrc.nist.gov/publications/PubsSPs.html

[21] Ross, Ron, et al., NIST SP 800-53, Revision 3, *Recommended Security Controls for Federal Information Systems and Organizations,* 2010, http://csrc.nist.gov/publications/PubsSPs.html

[22] Ross, Ron, et al., NIST SP 800-53A, Revision 1,*Guide for Assessing the Security Controls in Federal Information Systems and Organizations, Building Effective Security Assessment Plans,* 2010, http://csrc.nist.gov/publications/PubsSPs.html.

[23] Barker, William, NIST SP 800-59, *Guideline for Identifying an Information System as a National Security System*, 2003, http://csrc.nist.gov/publications/PubsSPs.html

[24] Barker, William, NIST SP 800-60, Revision 1, *Guide for Mapping Types of Information and Information systems to Security Categories*, 2008, http://csrc.nist.gov/publications/PubsSPs.html

[25] Souppaya, Murugiah, et al., NIST SP 800-70, Revision 1, *Security Configuration Checklists Program for IT Products – Guidance for Checklists Users and Developers*, 2005, http://csrc.nist.gov/publications/PubsSPs.html.

[26] Bowen, Pauline, et al., NIST SP 800-100, *Information Security Handbook: A Guide for Managers*, 2006, http://csrc.nist.gov/publications/PubsSPs.html.

[27] NIST Security Configurations Checklists Program for IT Products, http://checklists.nist.gov/

[28] Stamp, Jason, et al., *Common Vulnerabilities in Critical Infrastructure Control Systems*, Sandia National Laboratories, 2003, http://citeseerx.ist.psu.edu/viewdoc/download?doi=10.1.1.132.3264&rep=rep1&type=pdf.

[29] *SCADA Security - Advice for CEOs*, IT Security Expert Advisory Group (ITSEAG), http://www.ag.gov.au/agd/WWW/rwpattach.nsf/VAP/(930C12A9101F61D43493D44C70E84EAA)~SCADA+Security.pdf/$file/SCADA+Security.pdf

[30] Franz, Matthew, *Vulnerability Testing of Industrial Network Devices*, Critical Infrastructure Assurance Group, Cisco Systems, 2003, http://blogfranz.googlecode.com/files/franz-isa-device-testing-oct03.pdf

[31] Duggan, David, et al., *Penetration Testing of Industrial Control Systems*, Sandia National Laboratories, Report No SAND2005-2846P, 2005, http://www.sandia.gov/scada/documents/sand_2005_2846p.pdf.

[32] *21 Steps to Improve Cyber Security of SCADA Networks*, Office of Energy Assurance, U.S. Department of Energy, http://www.oe.netl.doe.gov/docs/prepare/21stepsbooklet.pdf.

[33] ISA-TR99.03.01: *Security Technologies for Industrial Automation and Control Systems*, ISA, 2007.

[34] *NISCC Good Practice Guide on Firewall Deployment for SCADA and Process Control Networks*, National Infrastructure Security Coordination Centre, London, 2005, http://www.cpni.gov.uk/docs/re-20050223-00157.pdf.

[35] Idaho National Laboratory, *Control Systems Cyber Security: Defense in Depth Strategies*, Homeland Security External Report # INL/EXT-06-11478, May 2006, http://csrp.inl.gov/Documents/Defense%20in%20Depth%20Strategies.pdf

[36] *The IAONA Handbook for Network Security – Draft/RFC v0.4*, Industrial Automation Open Networking Association (IAONA), Magdeburg, Germany, 2003.

[37] Idaho National Laboratory, *Common Control System Vulnerability*, Homeland Security External Report # INL/EXT-05-00993, November 2005, www.us-cert.gov/control_systems/pdf/csvul1105.pdf

[38] NIST SP 800-12, *An Introduction to Computer Security: The NIST Handbook*, 1995, http://csrc.nist.gov/publications/PubsSPs.html.

[39] Mell, Peter, et al., NIST SP 800-40 Version 2, *Creating a Patch and Vulnerability Management Program*, 2005, http://csrc.nist.gov/publications/PubsSPs.html.

[40] Scarfone, Karen, et al., NIST SP 800-115, Technical *Guide to Information Security Testing and Assessment*, 2008, http://csrc.nist.gov/publications/PubsSPs.html.

[41] Roback, Edward, NIST SP 800-23, *Guidelines to Federal Organizations on Security Assurance and Acquisition/ Use of Tested/Evaluated Products*, 2000, http://csrc.nist.gov/publications/PubsSPs.html

[42] Stoneburner, Gary, et al., NIST SP 800-27, *Engineering Principles for Information Security (A Baseline for Achieving Security), Revision A*, 2004, http://csrc.nist.gov/publications/PubsSPs.html

[43] Grance, Tim, et al., NIST SP 800-35, *Guide to Information Technology Security Services*, 2003, http://csrc.nist.gov/publications/PubsSPs.html.

[44] Grance, Tim, et al., NIST SP 800-36, *Guide to Selecting Information Technology Security Products*, 2003, http://csrc.nist.gov/publications/PubsSPs.html.

[45] Grance, Tim, et al., NIST SP 800-64, *Security Considerations in the Information System Development Life Cycle*, Revision 2, 2008, http://csrc.nist.gov/publications/PubsSPs.html

[46] Hash, Joan, et al., NIST SP 800-65, *Integrating IT Security into the Capital Planning and Investment Control Process*, 2005, http://csrc.nist.gov/publications/PubsSPs.html.

[47] SCADA and Control Systems Procurement Project, http://www.msisac.org/scada/

[48] Dray, James, et al., NIST SP 800-73-2, *Interfaces for Personal Identity Verification*, 2008, http://csrc.nist.gov/publications/PubsSPs.html.

[49] Wilson, Charles, et al., NIST SP 800-76, *Biometric Data Specification for Personal Identity Verification*, 2007, http://csrc.nist.gov/publications/PubsSPs.html.

[50] Kuhn, D. Richard, et al., NIST SP 800-46, *Security for Telecommuting and Broadband Communications*, 2002, http://csrc.nist.gov/publications/PubsSPs.html.

[51] Swanson, Marianne, et al., NIST SP 800-34, *Contingency Planning Guide for Information Technology Systems*, 2002, http://csrc.nist.gov/publications/PubsSPs.html.

[52] Burr, William, et al., NIST SP 800-63, *Electronic Authentication Guideline*, 2006, http://csrc.nist.gov/publications/PubsSPs.html.

[53] Bace, Rebecca, and Mell, Peter, NIST SP 800-31, *Intrusion Detection Systems*, 2001, http://csrc.nist.gov/publications/PubsSPs.html.

[54] Scarfone, Karen, and Mell, Peter, NIST SP 800-94, *Guide to Intrusion Detection and Prevention Systems (IDPS)*, 2007, http://csrc.nist.gov/publications/PubsSPs.html.

[55] Falco, Joe, et al., *Using Host-based Anti-virus Software on Industrial Control Systems: Integration Guidance and a Test Methodology for Assessing Performance Impacts*, NIST SP 1058, 2006, , http://www.nist.gov/manuscript-publication-search.cfm?pub_id=823596.

[56] Peterson, Dale, *Intrusion Detection and Cyber Security Monitoring of SCADA and DCS Networks*, ISA, 2004, http://whitepapers.techrepublic.com.com/whitepaper.aspx?&docid=126355&promo=100511.

[57] *Symantec Expands SCADA Protection for Electric Utilities*, http://www.symantec.com/about/news/release/article.jsp?prid=20050914_01

[58] Grance, Tim, et al., NIST SP 800-61, *Computer Security Incident Handling Guide*, 2004, http://csrc.nist.gov/publications/PubsSPs.html.

[59] Mell, Peter, et al., NIST SP 800-83, *Guide to Malware Incident Prevention and Handling*, 2005, http://csrc.nist.gov/publications/PubsSPs.html.

[60] Wilson, Mark, and Hash, Joan, NIST SP 800-50, *Building an Information Technology Security Awareness and Training Program*, 2003, http://csrc.nist.gov/publications/PubsSPs.html.

[61] Mix, S., *Supervisory Control and Data Acquisition (SCADA) Systems Security Guide*, EPRI, 2003.

[62] Karygiannis, Tom, and Owens, Les, NIST SP 800-48, *Wireless Network Security, 802.11, Bluetooth and Handheld Devices*, 2002, http://csrc.nist.gov/publications/PubsSPs.html.

[63] Frankel, Sheila, et al, NIST SP 800-97, *Guide to IEEE 802.11i: Establishing Robust Security Networks*, 2006, http://csrc.nist.gov/publications/PubsSPs.html.

[64] Federal Information Processing Standards Publication: FIPS 201-1, *Personal Identity Verification (PIV) of Federal Employees and Contractors*, NIST, 2006, http://csrc.nist.gov/publications/PubsSPs.html.

[65] Dray, James, et al, NIST SP 800-96, *PIV Card to Reader Interoperability Guidelines*, 2006, http://csrc.nist.gov/publications/PubsSPs.html.

[66] Polk, W., Timothy, et al, NIST SP 800-78, *Cryptographic Algorithms and Key Sizes for Personal Identity Verification*, 2007, http://csrc.nist.gov/publications/PubsSPs.html

[67] Souppaya, Murugiah, Kent, Karen, NIST SP 800-92, Guide to Computer Security Log Management, 2006, http://csrc.nist.gov/publications/PubsSPs.html.

[68] Jansen, Wayne, NIST SP 800-28, *Guidelines on Active Content and Mobile Code*, 2001, http://csrc.nist.gov/publications/PubsSPs.html.

[69] Chernick, Michael, et al, NIST SP 800-52, Guidelines for the Selection and Use of Transport Layer Security (TLS) Implementations, 2005, http://csrc.nist.gov/publications/PubsSPs.html

[70] Barker, Elaine, et al., NIST SP 800-56A, *Recommendation for Pair-Wise Key Establishment Schemes Using Discrete Logarithm Cryptography*, 2007, http://csrc.nist.gov/publications/PubsSPs.html.

[71] Baker, Elaine, et al., NIST SP 800-57, Recommendation for Key Management, 2006, Part 1, General: http://csrc.nist.gov/publications/PubsSPs.html, Part 2, Best Practices: http://csrc.nist.gov/publications/PubsSPs.html.

[72] Kuhn, D. Richard, et al., NIST SP 800-58, *Security Recommendations for Voice Over IP Systems*, 2005, http://csrc.nist.gov/publications/PubsSPs.html.

[73] Frankel, Sheila, et al, NIST SP 800-77, *Guide to IPsec VPNs*, 2005, http://csrc.nist.gov/publications/PubsSPs.html.

[74] Internet Security Glossary: RFC 4949, http://www.rfc-editor.org/rfc/rfc4949.txt

[75] Franz, Matthew, and Pothamsetty, Venkat, *ModbusFW Deep Packet Inspection for Industrial Ethernet*, Critical Infrastructure Assurance Group, Cisco Systems, 2004, http://blogfranz.googlecode.com/files/franz-niscc-modbusfw-may04.pdf.

[76] Duggan, David, *Penetration Testing of Industrial Control Systems*, Report SAND2005-2846P, Sandia National Laboratories, 2005, http://www.sandia.gov/scada/documents/sand_2005_2846p.pdf

[77] Kissel, Richard, et al., NIST SP 800-88, *Guidelines for Media Sanitization*, 2006, http://csrc.nist.gov/publications/PubsSPs.html.

Made in the USA
Coppell, TX
07 January 2021

47695686R10096